Exhibits and Displays

PRACTICAL GUIDES FOR LIBRARIANS

⌾ About the Series

This innovative series written and edited for librarians by librarians provides authoritative, practical information and guidance on a wide spectrum of library processes and operations.

Books in the series are focused, describing practical and innovative solutions to a problem facing today's librarian and delivering step-by-step guidance for planning, creating, implementing, managing, and evaluating a wide range of services and programs.

The books are aimed at beginning and intermediate librarians needing basic instruction/guidance in a specific subject and at experienced librarians who need to gain knowledge in a new area or guidance in implementing a new program/service.

⌾ About the Series Editors

The **Practical Guides for Librarians** series was conceived and edited by M. Sandra Wood, MLS, MBA, AHIP, FMLA, Librarian Emerita, Penn State University Libraries from 2014 to 2017.

M. Sandra Wood was a librarian at the George T. Harrell Library, the Milton S. Hershey Medical Center, College of Medicine, Pennsylvania State University, Hershey, PA, for over thirty-five years, specializing in reference, educational, and database services. Ms. Wood received an MLS from Indiana University and an MBA from the University of Maryland. She is a fellow of the Medical Library Association and served as a member of MLA's Board of Directors from 1991 to 1995.

Ellyssa Kroski assumed editorial responsibilities for the series beginning in 2017. She is the director of Information Technology at the New York Law Institute as well as an award-winning editor and author of thirty-six books including *Law Librarianship in the Digital Age* for which she won the AALL's 2014 Joseph L. Andrews Legal Literature Award. Her ten-book technology series, *The Tech Set*, won the ALA's Best Book in Library Literature Award in 2011. Ms. Kroski is a librarian, an adjunct faculty member at Drexel and San Jose State University, and an international conference speaker. She has just been named the winner of the 2017 Library Hi Tech Award from the ALA/LITA for her long-term contributions in the area of Library and Information Science technology and its application.

Recent books in the series include:

Exhibits and Displays

A Practical Guide for Librarians

Carol Ng-He
Patti Gibbons

PRACTICAL GUIDES FOR LIBRARIANS, NO. 72

ROWMAN & LITTLEFIELD
Lanham • Boulder • New York • London

Published by Rowman & Littlefield
An imprint of The Rowman & Littlefield Publishing Group, Inc.
4501 Forbes Boulevard, Suite 200, Lanham, Maryland 20706
www.rowman.com

6 Tinworth Street, London SE11 5AL, United Kingdom

British Library Cataloguing in Publication Information Available

Library of Congress Cataloging-in-Publication Data

Names: Ng-He, Carol, 1982- author. | Gibbons, Patti, 1972- author.
Title: Exhibits and displays : a practical guide for librarians / Carol Ng-He, Patti Gibbons.
Description: Lanham : Rowman & Littlefield, [2021] | Series: Practical guides for librarians ; 72 | Includes bibliographical references and index. | Summary: "This book guides readers to unleash their library's potential in making and hosting exhibits. Readers will gain a fundamental understanding about managing an exhibit program and a comprehensive view of planning and implementing exhibit projects, ranging from physical, traveling, to virtual"— Provided by publisher.
Identifiers: LCCN 2020047779 (print) | LCCN 2020047780 (ebook) | ISBN 9781538144039 (paperback) | ISBN 9781538144046 (epub)
Subjects: LCSH: Library exhibits—Handbooks, manuals, etc.
Classification: LCC Z717 .N55 2021 (print) | LCC Z717 (ebook) | DDC 021.7—dc23
LC record available at https://lccn.loc.gov/2020047779
LC ebook record available at https://lccn.loc.gov/2020047780

To my husband for his endless support, and to my children
for showing me nothing is impossible.
—Carol

To mom, thanks for making sure museums and
libraries were part of our family fun.
—Patti

Contents

Figures and Table

⊚ Figures

⊚ Table

Preface

Exhibits and displays allow libraries to create spaces for visitors to connect with collections and showcase a wide range of materials that immerse them in thematic learning environments. In recent years, exhibits and displays have increasingly become more prevalent and sophisticated. Going beyond show-and-tell, exhibits tie materials together with a curated voice that explores subjects, prompts critical thinking, and facilitates dialog with one another. Through exhibits and displays, libraries share more than books and text-based materials; they often highlight archival or rare items, artwork, audio recordings, and even hands-on experiments. Contemporary exhibits are created with the visitor's experience in mind, and librarians strive to educate, inspire, and delight visitors. However, most library curators, to some degree, are self-trained in the art of exhibit development and this book provides essential instruction, tips, and insight into exhibition design best practices that librarians need in order to produce crowd-pleasing exhibitions and displays.

In the following chapters, you will learn the full process of creating, implementing, and evaluating exhibits and displays in a library or information environment. The chapters are arranged in the sequential order that exhibit production generally takes, but each chapter can also be read as a stand-alone. While the guide considers both exhibits and displays, you will find heavier emphasis on exhibits due to their greater resource requirements. As the guide offers both a high-level view and specific action items in different areas in exhibit development, we encourage you to use this guide as a starting point to scale and customize your own planning for your next display projects.

Chapter 1 introduces readers to the central reasons why libraries create exhibits and displays and ways exhibit activities support professional development. Chapter 2 guides you to look critically at your institution's vision, mission, and goals, and examine different administrative aspects and resources that serve as the foundation of all the work you do in executing any exhibit plan. After you have a good grasp of those fundamental elements, chapter 3 shows you the strategies you need to get to know your audience and how you can create stories that resonate with them through exhibits. Once you find your story, chapter 4 covers ways you can write effective text and labels and provides real-world examples that you can learn from. Chapter 5 dives into the preparation and handling of collection items in physical exhibits and displays that are produced and fabricated in the library. You will also gain an understanding of the process and various dimensions of project management in developing an exhibit. Chapter 6 looks at how to plan and manage loans, traveling shows, and pop-up exhibits. As digital communications are increasingly visually oriented and customizable, more libraries experiment with digital exhibits. Chapter 7 looks at the opportunities and different types of digital exhibits with consideration of copyright issues, user experience, and accessible design interfaces. Chapter 8 looks at ways to market your work outside your library. It covers traditional and emerging promotional tactics and includes tips on how to use social media platforms effectively. In order to maximize the potential and reach of your exhibit, in chapter 9 the book surveys how to create engagement opportunities and programs that connect and tap into your audience's interests. The last chapter, chapter 10, gives an overview of what audience evaluation means to library exhibits, with examples from different types of libraries, and discusses how evaluation results can feed your next exhibit project. Throughout the guide, you will find various examples, vendor recommendations, and further readings to help build your exhibit tool kit.

As you embark on your journey creating library exhibits and displays, this book will help you create exhibits that are meaningful, inspiring, and thought-provoking for your community. If you are new to library exhibits, use this guide to empower yourself to venture out and expand your creative capacities. If you have experience in exhibit work, this guide will help you grow your exhibit program and better articulate your program's value.

With deep roots in exhibits at both public and academic libraries, we wrote the book to help librarians working in a variety of settings create exhibitions meaningful to their audiences and to provide practical approaches that meet the site-specific needs of diverse types and sizes of libraries. We have formal museum studies training and years of related professional experience that guide and inform our work. Our education and experience has enabled us to successfully register loans, oversee traveling exhibitions, manage collection care and preservation issues, and jumpstart meaningful outreach programs that expand audiences and build community support. Exhibits are fun, and an interactive way to celebrate your library's holdings, tell stories, and advance learning. They can speak to your visitors in ways traditional library services cannot, largely because exhibitions are unexpected and each is unique. We encourage you to dive into your collections, revisit them with fresh eyes to see what topics intrigue you, and look into the potential of your own community to imagine what you could develop into an exhibit theme. Stories lurk in your stacks and, with tips, instructions, and best practice recommendations that we have learned in museum studies classrooms and the onsite exhibit "laboratories" or "incubators" at our libraries, we want to support you as you bring them to life at your library.

While this book was written for librarians new to exhibitions with limited formal training, it also provides advice to experienced librarians looking to expand their exhibition programs. This book helps librarians create exhibits and displays in a variety of settings, including public, academic, school, and special libraries.

Acknowledgments

Juan Denzer, Engineering and Computer Science Librarian, Syracuse University Library, shared his considerable technological expertise in an essay on how to incorporate technology into exhibition interactives in chapter 8.

The following colleagues generously shared their experiences and reflections on exhibition evaluation in chapter 10:

Andrew Bullen, Information Technology Coordinator, Illinois State Library.

Amanda Cacich, Assistant Registrar and Exhibition Specialist, Newberry Library.

Doug Litts, Former Executive Director, Ryerson and Burnham Libraries, Art Institute of Chicago.

Megan Lotts, Art Librarian, Rutgers University Libraries.

Deborah Hicks, PhD, Assistant Professor, School of Information, San José University, reviewed and shared her editorial recommendations.

CHAPTER 1

Show It!

Why Libraries Create Exhibits and Displays

▷ Reasons to create library exhibits and displays

▷ Ways exhibit work supports professional development

Reasons to Create Library Exhibits and Displays

TRADITIONALLY VIEWED, LIBRARIES are text-driven places that generally are not thought of as sites for visual experiences. However, library exhibits flip this paradigm and highlight the visual side of your collections. Curating librarians harvest a range of holdings to tell stories, exemplify points, and engage visitors. Regardless of how big or small your exhibits or displays are, they showcase objects, images, literature, and informative text, and offer accessible and memorable experiences that spark curiosity, challenge assumptions, and engage library patrons in diverse perspectives.

Librarian Kerry O'Donnell at the Public Library of Brookline states, "Displays are useful for *informing* our community about special events and celebrations occurring in a given month, and they can be used to *promote* programs we have coming up. We make displays that *engage* in current trends and pop culture, *ask questions* that can entertain, or help us *improve* services we offer"[1] (emphasis added). As educational institutions, libraries use exhibits to advance their mission. Exhibits and displays are an important part of library services offered to the community and they showcase valuable library collections.

Library exhibits and displays are fundamentally visual experiences that enable libraries to achieve multiple learning and teaching goals. Exhibits and displays, as visual communications, promote artistic literacy and can facilitate creativity development for library patrons. It is a library's job to offer opportunities to experience art, so that the larger community develops an understanding and appreciation of art in its diverse forms.

Exhibits create bonding among community members and offer participants the space to see themselves and build empathy through visual storytelling and interactive components. Exhibits are catalysts of community activity and social change as library patrons take part in viewing, making, and dialoguing with other community members in the exhibits and associated programming and outreach activities.

Exhibits serve as the "hook" to pique a patron's interest and evoke excitement for library services. They create "buzz" in the community and work as effective public relations tools to increase awareness about the library and its services. In a way, exhibits allow the library "to speak in a new language to a wider audience" that might not have been done otherwise.[2]

Exhibits are often thought of in relation to museums, but library exhibits have a uniqueness that deserves its own attention. Unlike museums, people visit libraries mainly for access to books and information and often are surprised to encounter exhibits. Exhibits provide an added benefit to the visit. Therefore, exhibit librarians work in the world of opportunity, as they are in a position to create surprise and delight. Librarians can take advantage of this to guide discussion to people who come in without expectations or preconceived ideas. Librarians interested in developing exhibits often take on both curatorial and technical tasks—from selecting and arranging items to designing the panels and writing texts. Exhibit work presents many professional opportunities and challenges.

Ways Exhibit Work Supports Professional Development

Exhibits and displays offer the librarians great opportunities to develop and exercise various professional skills that can be applicable to other areas of their jobs. In order to make visually appealing displays, librarians must think creatively, master design software, and develop graphic design skills. The librarian needs exemplary project management, time management, and problem-solving skills to troubleshoot issues and create work plans to share with key stakeholders. To create effective exhibitions, librarians must hone written communication skills, as writing and editing item labels and the narrative exhibition didactics and copy for promotional materials are an important aspect of exhibit development. Exhibits offer librarians the opportunity to grow their collection-development skills as they identify subject strengths and opportunities to expand the library's holdings.

Other hidden but significant aspects of exhibit development work include personnel management, training and instruction, and public presentations. As part of community engagement, libraries may consider offering guided tours to groups that visit the exhibit, which presents an opportunity for volunteer or docent recruitment. From scoping the job responsibilities and training the volunteers, to evaluating the tour effectiveness, librarians are immersed in the world of developing and supervising staff and volunteers to support exhibit programs.

🌀 Definitions

- Display—a small selection of materials that are gathered as more of a show-and-tell rather than a group of items with a narrative or curated interpretation. The purpose of a display is to showcase something that may be visually appealing, new, or suggestive of an idea. The turnaround time from planning and execution is typically shorter than exhibits. Displays can be organized by one or a few people with a smaller or even no budget.
- Exhibit/Exhibition—a larger selection of materials with a deliberate story or a clear interpretation, sometimes immersive, interactive, and experiential. The turnaround time is longer than a display's as it involves a more complex production process from planning, designing, fabricating, prototyping, implementing, promoting, and evaluating. These require a greater extent of collaboration, funding, and contributors from different disciplines and expertise.

🌀 Key Points

- Library exhibits and displays serve multiple purposes and have significant impacts to individuals, the library, and the society
- Creating exhibits and displays help develop librarians' professional competencies that are transferred to other areas in their job

🌀 Notes

1. O'Donnell, Kerry. 2017. "How Do Library Displays Happen?" The Public Library of Brookline. Accessed September 1, 2020. https://www.brooklinelibrary.org/2017/04/20/how-do-library-displays-happen/.
2. Brim, Richenda. 2001. "From Custodians to Disseminators: Libraries and Digital Exhibitions." Howard Besser's webpage. Accessed September 1, 2020. http://besser.tsoa.nyu.edu/impact/f01/Papers/Brim/digi_ex.htm.

🌀 References

Brim, Richenda. 2001. "From Custodians to Disseminators: Libraries and Digital Exhibitions." September 1, 2020. http://besser.tsoa.nyu.edu/impact/f01/Papers?Brim/digi_ex.htm.

O'Donnell, Kerry. 2017. "How Do Library Displays Happen?" The Public Library of Brookline. September 1, 2020. https://www.brooklinelibrary.org/2017/04/20/how-do-library-displays-happen/.

🌀 Further Reading

Bedford, Leslie. 2014. *The Art of Museum Exhibits: How Story and Imagination Create Aesthetic Experiences.* New York: Routledge.

Smithsonian Institution. 2002. "The Making of Exhibits: Purpose, Structure, Roles and Process." Accessed September 1, 2020. https://www.si.edu/content/opanda/docs/rpts2002/02.10.makingexhibits.final.pdf.

Plan It!

Setting the Stage for Success

⊚ Align with Your Mission, Goals, and Values

BEFORE STARTING ANY WORK on creating a display or exhibit, you need to understand and be able to articulate how they connect with your larger organizational context. Organizational documents like your mission statement, strategic plan, and values statements offer an excellent starting place for matching your exhibit purpose with the needs of your library.

A mission is the organization's fundamental purpose and it answers the question, "Why does your library exist?" for all stakeholders, including staff, board, volunteers, community, and government agencies. Every organizational activity—from user services, to instructional programs, to collection practices—must point to the mission. The library's leadership articulates the mission and the statement can be updated to reflect the organization's current work and direction. Understanding your library's mission is critical and will help you speak the same language with everyone who works at your library, and it will enhance the performance effectiveness of your exhibits.

Your organization's strategic plan offers insights into the short-term goals of your library. It highlights strategies your library is undertaking to achieve its desired future and the plan delineates intended outcomes within a specific timeframe. You can use the strategic plan to help you advocate for exhibits and displays by integrating the library's strategic goals in your exhibit purpose. You may also want to consider if your department has its own sub-goals that complement the library's overall strategic plan. Aligning your ideas and goals for exhibits and displays to both your departmental and organizational aims will amplify your advocacy efforts.

Embrace and uphold your library's core values. They are fundamental beliefs and guiding principles that dictate the organizational culture and influence the decision-making process and behavioral expectations. The values can be found in explicit core values statements and can be gauged by examining past programs and services that the library has offered. Have your "pitch" reflect and support these values.

Keep in mind that sometimes libraries are not ready to take on displays and exhibits, so be prepared for objections and be realistic about what your library's current capacity can support. In this scenario, try to understand the reason behind the objections by having honest conversations with your supervisor. If the objection is due to budgetary constraints, explore external resources and funding opportunities that align with your library's goals and fit in the scope of your potential endeavors. Grants of various sizes are available locally and nationally through governmental agencies and philanthropic organizations. Research their websites and subscribe to their e-newsletters to learn more about programs and opportunities to support exhibit work. Also, identify allies outside of your library who might have encountered similar experiences. Optimize the power of your professional networks and memberships, share your challenges, and solicit feedback and suggestions on online discussion platforms—namely, the American Library Association's various community forums and the Art Libraries Society of North America Exhibitions Special Interest Group's listserv. Continue to expand your knowledge base on exhibit development for future reference. When the timing is right, share the information you have learned with your management and administration team and pitch your case again.

If staffing or staff time are concerns, research comparable libraries and their success stories. Examples can help illuminate the "return on investment" and real impacts exhibits have on communities.

If space limitations pose issues, think virtual. Please refer to chapter 7 for tips on creating digital exhibits.

As you begin to think about exhibits and displays at your library, ask yourself and your team these questions:

- What is my library's mission and how can exhibits help us advance our mission?
- What are the goals of my library's strategic plan and what role could exhibits and displays play?
- What are my library's core values and how can exhibits demonstrate them?

ⓖ Get Institutional Support

Support from the management, administration, and the governing board paves a solid ground in delivering your exhibit project. After you align your exhibit program objectives with your organization's mission, goals, and values, determine how exhibit planning is authorized.

Questions you should ask yourself include these:

- Does my library's leadership support the development of exhibits—financially and in personnel?
- What is the scope of exhibits the library can currently support?
- How is exhibit planning authorized?
- What is the approval process?

ⓖ Establish Policies and Procedures

Just like other operational areas in a library, policies and procedures set clear guidelines for staff when implementing exhibits. A policy outlines the objectives, scope, and responsibilities of how your displays and exhibits are determined and executed, while a procedure points out the detailed step-by-step instructions and workflow in line with the stated policy. Here is an example of the Exhibits Policy at the Arlington Heights Memorial Library:

EXHIBITS POLICY

This policy applies to exhibits selected, organized, sponsored, or hosted by the library. The library presents exhibits and exhibit experiences that provide opportunities for learning, enjoyment, inspiration, and cultural celebration to all audiences.

Exhibits include temporary and traveling exhibits. Exhibits may be sponsored by the library, including those created by community members, organizations (such as school districts), or professional artists. The location will be determined based on minimal impact to the library's everyday services, the intended audience, and other library needs for the space. The length of the exhibits may vary depending on space availability.

The selection criteria for library exhibits are as follows:

- Consistent with the library's vision and values
- Appeal to wide audiences and diverse community interests
- Potential for related programming and connection to library's collections and services
- Professional quality and condition of exhibit content
- Originality, accuracy, and artistic merit
- Accessibility
- Risk assessment
- Suitability to the library's physical spaces

- Cost
- Proposed return on investment
- Impact on staff and workload

Exhibits will be offered free of charge and open to the public. Library exhibit spaces cannot be used for political or commercial purposes or for the solicitation of business, profit, or fundraising, with the exception of fundraising that supports the library. The library may acknowledge exhibit sponsors as relevant.

Library Administration will review and approve or deny all recommended exhibits and related contract agreements.

Key questions to address when drafting a policy are as follows:

- What are the purposes of displays and exhibits at your library?
- What do exhibits mean at your library?
- Where are the exhibits located?
- When do you have exhibits and for how long?
- What are the selection criteria?
- Are displays and exhibits free and open to the public?
- What are the display and exhibit restrictions?
- Who in the library is authorized to review and approve/disapprove exhibit plans?

When drafting the procedures, ask yourself these questions:

- Who needs to be involved in the discussion?
- What kind of customer support system needs to be in place before the procedure is implemented? For example, does an online application form need to be created? If so, how will it be tested?
- Are there other libraries that have done similar work you can reference?
- How will staff be informed about the policy and procedures? Will training occur once or on a regular basis?
- How will the policy and procedures be updated?

⑥ Set Exhibit Scope

There are various determining factors to charter an exhibit project: budget, timeline, space requirement (physical or virtual), size (physical dimensions or digital storage volume), format (interactive or viewing only), staff and volunteer roles, collaboration opportunities (internal and/or external), and other special considerations. Major factors will be explained in the following sections.

It is imperative to involve key stakeholders at your library to address the above factors. Involve them in your initial planning discussions and consult with them often to capture essential information in order to make sure your work aligns with your library's goals.

⊚ Allocate a Budget

Once you determine the exhibit, research and create an itemized budget for the exhibit. Determine what expenses would be absorbed by your department or shared across other departments or collaborating organizations.

Examples of exhibit expenses include the following:

- Supplies: adhesive, consumables, cleaning supplies, paint
- Loan: rental fees
- Technology: electronic hardware, software
- Furniture: display cases, shelving units, additional seating and tables
- Services: graphic design and printing, installation and deinstallation assistance, moving services, off-site storage, translation
- Others: shipping, guestbooks, and evaluation materials

In addition, when you develop your budget, you may want to think beyond your immediate exhibit plans and consider long-term financial needs. Questions you should ask yourself include the following:

- How many exhibits do we want to have in a given year?
- What kinds of services and/or supplies do we need for any specific exhibit?
- What are the costs for staff professional development opportunities on exhibits?

⊚ Develop Staff and Volunteers

Continuing education enhances exhibit quality and library visitor experience. Talent development is a year-round endeavor. As noted, staff participation in conferences, workshops, webinars, and other learning opportunities organized by external professional associations or groups should be budgeted to encourage staff to stay abreast of the best practices, trends, standards, and tips on exhibit development.

Internal and peer education can also be valuable. Through departmental meetings or interdepartmental training, librarians can develop new awareness of resources and databases that could be useful for exhibit organizing, such as grant writing, technical training on design software, or project management application. Not only does peer training boost camaraderie and work morale, but it also helps solicit more staff buy-in on exhibits—especially if exhibits are still newly introduced to the library.

⊚ Identify Collaboration Opportunities

The best exhibits are often a collaborative effort. They require diverse skill sets and expertise in order to present a quality and well-rounded educational experience for the audience. Preparing room for collaborations in each stage of the exhibit yields great benefits.

Advisory Group and Production Team

Consider forming an exhibit advisory group, made up of staff from all parts of the organization, to coordinate, plan, implement, and assess the exhibits and displays. Consider including representatives who will also likely be on your production team, such as graphic designers, IT technicians, communications and marketing staff, librarians, and frontline staff. The skills each of these representatives bring will not only be vital for mounting the exhibit, but will also ensure that a range of considerations will be addressed during the planning phase.

Exhibit Selection

Opening up dialogue across the library can be an effective way to get internal buy-in, as well as to identify strengths, weaknesses, risks, and opportunities that potential exhibits may bring to the library in both the immediate- and long-term periods. Using the policy as your base, consult with your colleagues—especially those in the frontlines, who have gained direct feedback from the patrons—to learn more about community interests. Consult your exhibits advisory group on potential exhibit themes. This collaborative approach can help departments to get to know each other's needs, goals, and organizational purpose more closely. In short, it promotes a more holistic perspective of the library operations for participating staff members. When developing your exhibit lineup, survey and revisit any expressed interest in an exhibit from community members.

Contract Negotiation

In the case of traveling exhibits, once an exhibit is recommended, work with the finance team or whomever handles legal matters for contract negotiations. In terms of exhibit promotion, it is wise to gather feedback from communications and marketing teams to examine any red flags or precautionary areas. For smaller libraries where staff bears multiple duties, have your senior staff members review the contract.

Community Partnerships

Leverage existing resources and network to strengthen your exhibit content and potential. For public libraries, explore the interest of local community partners such as schools, daycare centers, government agencies, hospitals, senior centers, local businesses, and perhaps more relevantly, museums and historical societies. Displays and exhibits can help to promote charitable causes, special events, and local resources. Some exhibits present great opportunities for joint programming. For example, a public library can partner with local schools to display students' artwork in their space.

Community partners for academic libraries may include faculty, research institutes, campus departments, and individual students and student groups. Exhibits and exhibit spaces in libraries can be "a great way to connect with the overall campus community as well as a way to promote cross-disciplinary collaboration."[1] Developing exhibits in collaboration with the academic community allows library liaisons to form deeper and more meaningful connections with the individuals and departments they work with. In turn, librarians can also learn more about the research needs of their students, faculty, and staff. For example, Megan Lotts, an art librarian from Rutgers University, has worked with fine art students to help them mount their first solo exhibits. Megan assisted the student in creating press releases and publicity while the student was responsible for exhibition installation and deinstallation. The collaboration transforms the art library into a space for experiential learning and supports students' career development.

Assess Your Space

Once there is institutional support to organize exhibits, and you have determined your exhibit plans, evaluate the type of spaces that are available to you. Questions to consider are these:

- What are the spaces available for exhibitions for multi-month and pop-up exhibits? Are there shelves, cases, common area, walls, and so forth?
- What additional amenities are available in these spaces that support exhibits and programs?
- What kind of space do we need to create to meet future exhibit and display opportunities?
- Does my library have the budget and people to support the building or purchasing of additional cases and walls?
- Does my library have space to store and care for freestanding cases and/or moveable display walls?
- Are we ready to display materials that require special environmental protections or additional security?

Types of Spaces Needed for Exhibits and Displays

Physical

The physical spaces can include built-in environments and supplemental spaces. Built-in environments are unmovable preexisting structures. For example, galleries, glass display cases, common or multipurpose areas, book shelves, and hallways. Except for galleries and display cases that are dedicated and enclosed space for exhibitions and displays, other spaces are often shared with non-exhibit functions. In some cases, librarians will need to work with an open floor plan to creatively place exhibit elements. For larger scale exhibits, ceiling heights and the flexibility of lighting controls and lighting fixtures would be another element to consider in planning. Supplemental spaces may include freestanding display cases and walls that could be used as a stand-alone display space or as an additional element in an exhibit.

Infrastructure to take into consideration when developing exhibit spaces include the availability of power outlets, the position of lights, whether shelving units are flexible/removable, temperature and humidity controls, and security capacities. For displays and exhibits that include rare book items, facility and environmental requirements must be met. See chapter 5 for more information on preservation concerns.

When exhibits are not on view, consider storage of the freestanding gallery furniture. If the library desires to purchase or build their own items, cost and labor are important considerations.

Figure 2.1. Installation view of *Discovery, Collection, Memory: The Oriental Institute at 100* exhibition. *Carol Ng-He.*

Examples

The *Discovery, Collection, Memory: The Oriental Institute at 100* exhibition was on view in the University of Chicago Library's Special Collections Research Center gallery—a space dedicated to rotating rare book and archival exhibitions (see figure 2.1).

The *Inclusion Awareness Month* display was on view in a built-in glass display case at the Arlington Heights Memorial Library's Kids' World (see figure 2.2). The display featured the library's sensory-friendly collections and resources on accessibility available for patrons.

The Smithsonian Institution Traveling Exhibition Service's *Earth from Space* exhibit consisted of elements displayed on two freestanding Z-shaped walls built by the hosting library's staff. The exhibit showcases twenty color, satellite images of the Earth from the moon, video clips and sound bites from NASA's website, and a backdrop for photo-taking produced in-house by library staff (see figure 2.3).

Pop-Ups

Pop-up exhibits and displays usually last for a few hours to a week or so. Treated as a temporary exhibit, this kind of display typically needs basic furniture—as simple as a folding table and possibly a tent, if outdoors. This display can serve as an excellent off-site

Figure 2.2. *Inclusion Awareness Month* display. *Carol Ng-He.*

outreach interactive with minimal budget and staffing resource requirements. Pop-ups also allow high flexibility for the library's staff to expand collaborations with allied organizations in a short amount of time.

Example

The Penn Museum Library staff created *Off the Shelf*, a series of pop-up exhibits that were scheduled for one hour on the last Friday afternoon of every month (see figure 2.4). The

Figure 2.3. Installation view of *Earth from Space* exhibition. *Carol Ng-He.*

series aimed to invite the Penn community and Penn Museum visitors to "learn about Penn Libraries holdings through the lens of a tailored theme," prompt visitors to "make historical conversations relevant to modern discourse," and "inspire undergraduates to engage critically with the materials" to reveal the potential for research.[2]

Mobile and Off-Site Exhibits

Mobile and off-site exhibits come in two varieties. Sometimes they are library-developed pop-ups that can be displayed "on the road." Here, libraries bring a selection of collections and "pop them up" in unorthodox spaces, such as a community center, mall, or public gathering places outside of the library. Other times, libraries serve as a host site for a traveling exhibit developed by external groups or organizations.

Examples

The Sketchbook Project of Brooklyn Art Library hosts mobile exhibitions with the Mobile Library, an interactive art exhibition on wheels that carries a selection of sketchbooks to museums, galleries, festivals, and academic institutions across North America.[3]

Salina Public Library in Kansas City hosted the University of Kansas Natural History Museum's Pop-Up Mobile Museum for four hours on a summer Friday afternoon.

Figure 2.4. Monthly pop-up exhibit. *Courtesy of the University of Pennsylvania Libraries.*

A display of ninety species, a dinosaur skull cast, and a storybook on prehistoric creatures were on display. Hands-on paleontology activities engaged children and families at the event.[4]

Special Considerations

Different exhibits and displays have different environmental requirements for the preservation of the items on display. Some have more strict requirements than others—in particular, for the displays and exhibits of rare books and items. In the case of loan or traveling exhibits, lending institutions usually have set guidelines prior to a contract being signed. Typically, areas such as the following are addressed:

- Temperature control
- Humidity
- Light control
- Staging and storage
- Security
- Shipping and receiving
- Food and drink

See chapters 5 and 6 for more details on each of these areas. Generally, questions to ask when considering hosting an exhibit or displaying sensitive materials include the following:

- Can my library maintain the standard temperature and humidity ranges?
- Can we meet the lighting requirement?
- Can my library provide the level of security required?
- Does my library have a secured storage area for temporary exhibition objects, as well as for crates and packing materials?
- Does my library have an exhibit prep area to receive, repack, and stage exhibit materials?
- What is the maximum size vehicle my loading area can accommodate?
- Can the exhibition area be locked and secure during closing hours?

Your library's facilities and security staff can be an excellent resource for addressing these questions.

🌀 Definitions

- Goals—the end results to which effort is directed toward
- Mission—the organization's fundamental purpose; it answers the question, "Why does your library exist?"
- Policy—a statement of intent and a course of actions that is adopted by the governing body within an organization and implemented as a procedure or protocol
- Procedure—a document that describes who, what, where, when, and how to support the implementation of a policy
- Values—the fundamental beliefs and guiding principles that dictate the organizational culture and influence the decision-making process and behavioral expectations

🌀 Key Points

- Before any planning begins, make sure the purpose of the exhibit aligns with your library's mission, goals, and values
- Get support from your organization's leadership to implement your exhibit plan
- Establish policies and procedures for exhibits to give clarity to your library's stakeholders and maintain corporate accountability
- Determine the scope of your exhibit to set the perimeter of your project planning
- Continuously seek opportunities for yourself and peers to develop skills and knowledge to enhance exhibit quality and keep up with the industry's best practices
- Identify collaboration opportunities to maximize the effectiveness and impact of your exhibits
- Consider other special requirements—such as temperature, humidity, lighting control, staging and storage, and security—in hosting traveling exhibits

🌀 Notes

1. Lotts, Megan. 2016. "Building Bridges, Creating Partnerships, and Elevating the Arts: The Rutgers University Art Library Exhibition Spaces." *College & Research Libraries News*. 77 (5): 226–30.

2. Stiteler, Gretchen. 2019. "Penn Museum Library Shares Rare Books in Monthly Pop-Up Exhibits." *Penn Libraries News*. Accessed September 1, 2020. https://www.library.upenn.edu/blogs/libraries-news/2019/05/29/5928.

3. The Sketchbook Project. "Work with the Sketchbook Project." Accessed September 1, 2020. https://www.sketchbookproject.com/exhibitions.

4. *Salina Journal*. 2019. "Salina Public Library to Host Pop-Up Mobile Museum." Accessed September 1, 2020. https://www.salina.com/news/20190703/salina-public-library-to-host-pop-up-mobile-museum.

⊚ References

Lotts, Megan. 2016. "Building Bridges, Creating Partnerships, and Elevating the Arts: The Rutgers University Art Library Exhibition Spaces." *College & Research Libraries News.* 77(5): 226–30.

Salina Journal. "Salina Public Library to Host Pop-Up Mobile Museum." September 1, 2020. https://www.salina.com/news/20190703/salina-publiclibrary-to-host-pop-up-mobil-museum.

Stiteler, Gretchen. 2019. "Penn Museum Library Shares Rare Books in Monthly Pop-Up Exhibits." September 1, 2020. https://www.library.upenn.edu/blogs/libraries-news/2019/05/29/5928.

The Sketchbook Project. "Work with The Sketchbook Project." September 1, 2020. https://www.sketchbookproject.com/exhibitions.

Tell It!

Know Your Audience and Find Your Story

PEOPLE VISIT LIBRARIES PRIMARILY for books and typically are not focused on visiting for your exhibits or displays. That certainly does not mean they will not enjoy your exhibits, but you need to entice and attract people while they visit the library. As your exhibit program grows, you will build in expectations that keep visitors coming back and be increasingly on their radar. Unlike museums that attract people for their exhibitions, libraries operate on opportunity and often surprise visitors with displays that inform and inspire. Your work as an exhibition librarian adds value to the organizational mission and enhances a visitor's experience.

Understanding Your Audience

No one is more expert than you to gauge and assess your own library patrons. Working and interacting with them positions you to have insights into their interests, likes, and dislikes. Knowing the materials that circulate most often, fielding reference questions, and listening to their requests gives you a perspective that can help you select exhibition topics and shape how you present materials to appeal to your audience. As a seasoned professional, you have a very accurate sense of your visitors' needs, interests, and levels of engagement.

Consider Your Setting

Do you work in an academic library where visitors are driven by formal studies and curriculum? Are you working in a public library that acts as an entertainment hub and portal for a range of life services? Or are you seated in a corporate library where your patrons rely on your materials to complete professional projects? Thinking about the people you interact with on a daily basis and considering what drives them to use your library provides you with a degree of insight into their interests. Also, consider what a typical visit looks like at your library. Are visitors rushed and arrive for a well-defined list of materials? Or do they explore the setting and collections? Thinking about the pace and aim of your patrons' visits can inform how much information they may be interested in when seeing a display or exhibit.

If the range of people who come to your library is vast, take a step back and consider who you think would most appreciate a particular exhibition. Your target audience can and will change; your exhibit focus steers selection in some sense. It is fine to narrow the scope of your topic and allow yourself not to feel obliged to reach *everyone* who visits.

Who Are Your Visitors?

Thinking about your audience, their visitation patterns, their interests, their point of views, and their readiness to learn, can be tremendously helpful and can help your message reach its target effectively. As you are developing your exhibits and displays, imagine who you are talking to and trying to reach. As you identify topics, select materials, and write interpretive text, you might even envision a theoretical archetypical visitor—perhaps a patron you helped or a composite of types of people you have interacted with in the past.

Consider Visitor Demographics

Reviewing demographics can help you think about your audience and develop exhibits that reflect their life experiences and interests. Creating exhibits that speak to people or pique their interest helps you engage groups and get your messages heard. With your exhibit program, take time to reflect on your audience. How old are your visitors? What is their reading level? Do people have physical or mental limitations? Vision impairment? Are they experts in a particular topic or open to lifelong learning? Is English their second language? Are your patrons faith based or politically oriented? Knowing your audience helps you select topics that interest them and informs the ways you tell stories so narratives are compelling and understandable and consider the perspectives of your unique community.

Demographic Considerations

- Age
- Gender
- Race, nationality

- Marital status
- Occupations
- Income level
- Educational level
- Disabilities
- Affiliations—religious, political, organizational ties

Exhibits, as an outreach tool, can help your library connect with select populations. Are you trying to increase visits with a particular demographic? Creating exhibits geared to their interests may engage these constituencies. If, for example, you want to grow your young adult audience or provide value to stakeholders of a law library with your offerings, crafting exhibits for these groups can help you connect with and engage these audiences in a fun way that highlights relevant collections.

Advisory Panel

Depending on the size of your exhibit program, and the time you can devote, you might consider developing a community advisory panel to discuss exhibit ideas and get to know your audience better.[1] Recruiting members from your constituency can be beneficial in multiple ways. Membership can engage users such as teen reviewers at a public library or graduate students at an academic library and help develop topics or perhaps test item selection, and these people, in turn, can help you promote and publicize the exhibit through their networks.

Collection SWOT Analysis

There are a million stories to tell at a library, and when turning to your collections as source materials to build exhibits from, librarians are wading in infinitely fertile grounds. When planning your exhibit schedule and considering which subjects to develop, librarians can turn to their collection strengths to find topics to explore that will inspire visitors and promote collection holdings. Furthermore, through your daily work with visitors, you have a well-founded sense of what types of materials they read and what interests them. Your observations provide you with accurate insights into topics that appeal to your library's visitors.

SWOT: Strengths

SWOT analysis—strengths, weaknesses, opportunities, and threats—is a matrix used in many contexts. In terms of a framework to define and guide exhibition selection, librarians can look at their collections as a whole and consider what their particular top strengths are at their library. What makes your library's collection unique? What are your institutional collection strengths? What topics, subjects, and areas do you have the deepest collection holdings in? You very likely will find success developing exhibits about these topics. Lead with your strengths and create exhibits using collection gems, or parts of your holdings that are particularly deep, complete, or unique. When brainstorming potential exhibitions, write out a list of your most prominent collections, consider which holdings are distinctive, and examine data that identifies your top circulating materials.

SWOT: Weaknesses

Conversely, knowing your collecting weaknesses will show you areas to avoid. If your holdings are incomplete or do not cover subject areas, you are not on solid footing for developing exhibits for topics outside of your collecting area. For instance, if you are working in an art library, your collection focus on art-related topics is a strength that general libraries cannot rival. Developing exhibits about artists, art genres, and art-related movements capitalizes on a strength. Considering exhibits about non-art related topics such as transportation and numismatics is a little out of step and would likely result in a weaker exhibition experience, or require you to purchase or borrow materials for the exhibition. Often, when you do not have resources to tell the story, chances are you identified an exhibit theme not apt to be explored in your setting.

SWOT: Opportunities

Thinking about your collections and connections with your patrons, exhibits present an exciting opportunity to convey knowledge and to inspire and direct thinking and action. People are listening, and you can say something that increases awareness, informs, or even prompts a call to action. Through books and words, you can show excellence, beauty, understanding, and in some cases, a need for change.

- Did your library recently acquire a new collection?
- Have there been recent scientific discoveries in a topic or are fields trending in general social interest where you hold collections?
- Are there milestone anniversaries about to happen—such as a prolific author's birthday, anniversary of landmark legislation, or regional plans to commemorate important community events—that provide an opportunity for a discussion on a topic?
- Do your collections speak to the interests of specific audiences, clubs, or groups?
- If your audience is open to whimsy, perhaps using national food holidays or pet days could launch fun exhibitions or a rotation of impromptu displays

SWOT: Threats

As experts in particular fields, subjects, or disciplines, forgoing exhibits on topics puts you at a disadvantage to educate or reach your audiences. Not creating exhibits is a missed opportunity that leads to a void.

Taking time to survey exhibitions at nearby peer institutions where there is overlap with your visitors can identify exhibition themes covered in your community. Though this certainly does not mean you cannot discuss the topic, you will need to find new ground. By surveying the work of peers, you minimize the risk of retelling stories. To some degree, people may be less interested in seeing an exhibit that explores a topic they have already seen on display.

Idea Bank

Once you complete a SWOT analysis, it is an excellent time to create an idea bank. Brainstorm and dream about interesting future exhibits that highlight collection strengths and take advantage of opportunities. Jot down topics. You do not need to flesh out complete ideas at this stage, but take time to explore. Consider everything. Great exhibit ideas have a way of percolating and coming into focus with time. Formal brainstorming sessions can be very fruitful when you collaborate with others. You might consider establishing an exhibition team with select colleagues and meet at set intervals to project and look ahead. You will very likely get inspirations and ideas for exhibits outside of your formal planning sessions. Be sure to recognize your inspired moments and write down your ideas in your exhibit idea bank.

◎ Curating and Exhibit Development

After selecting and refining your exhibition topic, you will develop the idea by researching the subject, considering your audience, defining learning expectations, selecting items that attract the eye and inspire curiosity, and interpreting the holdings to illustrate your thesis.[2]

These are the main parts of a curator's work developing an exhibit:

1. Selecting a theme
2. Finding your unique story or angle
3. Considering your audience and establishing learning objectives
4. Selecting items and their arrangement
5. Writing interpretive text that informs and tells a cohesive story

Selecting a Theme

As curator, and master storyteller, you begin with a story needing to be told. Consider, what is it about the topic that fascinates you? Is the story fresh, interesting, and something your visitors need to experience? As you flesh out the exhibit's themes and mission, take time to explicitly define what you would like the visitor to learn, and consider what you would like them to do with the information. This will guide how you execute your item selection, text, and overall exhibition development experience.

Finding Your Unique Story or Angle

When brainstorming potential exhibit subjects, look for an interesting angle about a topic. Is it an age-old story you feel needs to be told to a new generation? Has there been new research in an old topic? Did your library receive a gift of materials in a new collecting area? The more specific your exhibition's scope is, the better. Focused themes tell new and insightful stories that demonstrate the power of your library's materials.

A well-defined topic helps you tell a more compelling and clear narrative. Tackling broad subjects such as World War II, Prohibition, or the Space Race in a single exhibition is nearly impossible and your visitors will likely already know the basics about these topics. Your exhibit should tell them something they did not know or ask them to consider a particular aspect, subset of the topic, or a lesser-known angle that tells a smaller story. More defined stories help you highlight your library's unique holdings and impart a message that visitors can "digest" during their visits.

Another strategy to help you narrow a broad topic is to look at the subject during a specific timeframe—say, British pop music in the 1980s. Another is to examine a subject from the point of view of a particular group—for instance, Latino activist murals rather than a broader topic of urban street art. Like catalogers who refine the subject specificity when assigning call numbers, consider how specific you can go to deepen your exhibit focus.

Consider Your Audience and Establish Learning Objectives

As you develop your exhibit, have your audience in mind. Envision your theoretical archetypical visitor and think about what you want to tell that person. Knowing their interests and ways they generally interact with your organization helps you write text and select items particularly for them.

Exhibits and displays are powerful and palatable ways to impart knowledge, "edutain," commemorate events, and raise awareness of issues and causes. As a curator developing an exhibit, always ask yourself, "What do I want people to do with the information I'm providing?"

As you work, consider the following:

- Do you want to inform?
- Are you commemorating an event or anniversary?
- Do you want visitors to reflect?
- Are you seeking change and want people to react?
- Do you want people to appreciate aesthetic or literary accomplishments?

In thinking about your ideal response to information and identifying how you would like visitors to react to your exhibit, you will take a different stance in your writing and item selection. If you are looking to entertain, fanciful items may appeal more than standard-issue ones and your text will be punchy and tell stories that inspire or create joy. If you intend to coax action, you will select items that scream urgency and that support your theme unequivocally, and the tone of your text will be direct and unambiguous. When you are developing exhibits, plan how you want people to respond. From there, you can shape the tone of your message and use your big-picture end goal to guide your item selection.

After establishing the overall tone and mission, it is helpful to parse out specific learning objectives for each exhibit. What three key messages do you want your visitor to take away after seeing your exhibit? For example, in a show focused on medical illustrations about midwifery in 1850, with an overall mission to educate people 170 years later, perhaps the three key messages would be these:

- Midwives provided medical and emotional support to women during childbirth
- Birthing equipment of the day was limited to stethoscopes, clamps, and forceps
- Mortality rates for both mother and child were much greater than today

Item Selection and Arrangement

As curator, you want to select the items that best exemplify your point, illustrate your learning objectives, and capture the tone of your message. If choosing between two similar items, consider the items' condition and visual appeal. Which is in the best physical shape? Does one have more visual allure than the other? Does one present any challenges for mounting or display? Is one larger and easier to see? Are there copy-specific features that would interest people, such as an elaborate binding or inscription? Beyond visuals and physical characteristics, when selecting items, challenge yourself and ask whether the item most clearly demonstrates your point.

When planning exhibits, curators need to consider arrangement of items and how they would like visitors to move through the exhibit. Do you want to tell your story linearly? Would you like to discuss your topic in categories or parts? Do certain materials need to be paired together to explain a message or illustrate a point? Thinking about the overall underlying sequencing guides your writing and informs item selection.

Writing Interpretive Text That Informs and Tells a Cohesive Story

Curating exhibits takes on a role of authority. The information you are disseminating must be factual. As curator, you have to vet your stories, research your subject thoroughly, and fact-check to ensure accuracy in your exhibit's message and information. Curators should take a balanced approach and discuss issues from different points of view. If discussing a topic with controversial aspects, cover multiple perspectives in your text. Visitors trust your voice as being an authority on the subject, and due diligence is required.

As a writer, you will describe individual items, but you also need to explain why they are in the exhibit and displayed with other items. Tell the who, why, what, where, when, and how. Focus on the way items fit into your narrative and serve as examples of your overarching story. As curator, you are interpreting history and telling a story through the books, papers, and objects you bring together and write about. Some connections may be obvious, but others require you to summarize pairings and point out the significance of associations.

During your writing and exhibition development, resist urges to dive too deeply and exhaustively tell visitors *everything* about a subject. Remain selective. This is an opportunity to highlight, not to dissertate. If you include too many examples, repeat messages, or complicate a story, visitors will likely tire and walk away. Stay focused and keep coming back to your main messages and learning objectives in order to select and interpret materials effectively and tell a streamlined and focused narrative.

◉ Examples

The following are examples of exhibits about Beat poetry, but the focuses are different and tell two unique stories about the American literary movement established and popularized during the 1950s.

Example 1

The first example is a walk-through on how the *City Lights Pocket Poets Series 1955–2005* exhibit was developed at the University of Chicago Library's Special Collections Research Center.[3]

STARTING WITH A BROAD TOPIC, THE THEME NARROWED

Poetry > Modern US Poetry > Beat Poetry > Publishing Beat Poetry > City Lights Press's Influence and Coverage of Beat Poets

Knowing that poetry, modern American poetry, and even Beat poetry were too broad of topics to tackle, the curatorial team selected an interesting angle within the Beat poetry genre. Making a bit of a left turn, they explored an idea to focus on publishing, and the brainstorm led to City Lights, an independent bookstore and press in San Francisco that ardently supported Beat authors.

In the exhibit about City Lights Press's influence on Beat poetry, curators discussed poetry (the wide subject) indirectly, but assumed visitors would come to the exhibit with some understanding of poetry and, to some extent also, the Beat genre. Curators focused their attention on the aspect of publishing these poets' work and the influences City Lights had in the dissemination and promotion of the genre. The exhibit covered lesser-known ground that intrigued its visitors. The exhibit explored the work of top poets in the genre, their publishing stories, and the scope and influence of City Lights Pocket Poet series.

Example 2

In 2007, the New York Public Library exhibited *Kerouac at Bat: Fantasy Sports and the King of the Beats*, curated by Isaac Gewirtz.[4] The exhibit told the story of twentieth-century American poet and novelist Jack Kerouac drawing on their published book holdings and their manuscript archival papers. Rather than retell stories related to the author's published literary works, the library focused its exhibit on the influential author's private life and hobbies. Jack Kerouac was deeply interested in baseball and, as a fan, created zines of imagined team contests. He wrote extensive notes and projected game results. He illustrated his fanzines and studded them with copious statistical notes.

The NYPL exhibit told the story of a fanzine publication as produced by a national literary treasure known and celebrated for his literary talents. It was an unfamiliar perspective of Kerouac's biography, using collection materials to document his life experience and deep hobbyist interest, while also using Kerouac's artifacts to explain gaming and fantasy sports betting. The NYPL expertly used its unique collections to tell a virtually unknown story about an American literary icon, even noting that contemporary poetic luminaries and associates like Allen Ginsberg were unaware of Kerouac's obsession with baseball during their lifetimes. The exhibit was an opportunity to highlight the library's unique holdings (the Kerouac Papers), as well as an occasion to educate visitors on an unknown aspect of a prominent literary figure's personal life.

◎ Definitions

- Curation—the process of selecting, organizing, and interpreting materials for an exhibition
- Edutainment—entertainment intended to be educational in nature
- SWOT analysis—a self-reflection process to identify organizational strengths, weaknesses, opportunities, and threats

◎ Key Points

- Your expertise and working relationship with patrons will help you immensely to understand your audience, their interests, and their expectations
- Create exhibits that highlight collection strengths at your library

- Be selective and narrow the focus of your exhibition theme
- Tell fresh, factual stories that support defined learning objectives

⊚ Notes

1. Lord, Barry, and Gail Dexter Lord, eds. 2002. *The Manual of Museum Exhibitions.* Walnut Creek, CA: AltaMira Press, 32–34.

2. Smithsonian Institution. [2016]. *Museum on Main Street: Storytelling Toolkit.* Washington, DC: Smithsonian Institution. PDF e-publication. Accessed September 1, 2020. https://museum onmainstreet.org/search/node/storytelling%20toolkit.

3. *City Lights Pocket Poets Series 1955–2005: From the Collection of Donald A. Henneghan.* October 1, 2005–January 1, 2006. Special Collections Research Center, University of Chicago Library, Chicago.

4. Gewirtz, Isaac. 2009. *Kerouac at Bat: Fantasy Sports and the King of the Beats.* New York: New York Public Library.

⊚ References

City Lights Pocket Poets Series 1955–2005: From the Collection of Donald A. Henneghan. October 1, 2005–January 1, 2006. Special Collections Research Center, University of Chicago Library, Chicago.

Gewirtz, Isaac. 2009. *Kerouac at Bat: Fantasy Sports and the King of the Beats.* New York: New York Public Library.

Lord, Barry, and Gail Dexter Lord, eds. 2002. *The Manual of Museum Exhibitions.* Walnut Creek, CA: AltaMira Press.

Smithsonian Institution. [2016]. *Museum on Main Street: Storytelling Toolkit.* Washington, DC: Smithsonian Institution. PDF e-publication. Accessed September 1, 2020. https://museum onmainstreet.org/search/node/storytelling%20toolkit.

⊚ Further Reading

Ambrose, Timothy and Crispin Paine. 2012. *Museum Basics.* New York: Routledge.

Bridal, Tessa. 2013. *Effective Exhibit Interpretation and Design.* Lanham, MD: AltaMira Press.

Brubach, Holly. 2019. *Masters at Work: Becoming a Curator.* New York: Simon & Schuster.

Dean, David. 2000. *Museum Exhibition: Theory and Practice.* New York: Routledge.

Durbin, Gail, eds. 1996. *Developing Museum Exhibitions for Lifelong Learning.* London: The Stationary Office.

Hansens, Malene Vest, Anne Folke Henningsen, and Anne Gregersen, eds. 2019. *Curatorial Challenges: Interdisciplinary Perspectives on Contemporary Curating.* New York: Routledge.

Malm, Magdalena, ed. 2017. *Curating Context: Beyond the Gallery and into Other Fields.* Stockholm: Art and Theory Publishing.

Matassa, Freda. 2014. *Organizing Exhibitions: A Handbook for Museums, Libraries, and Archives.* London: Facet.

Serrell, Beverly. 2006. *Judging Exhibitions: A Framework for Assessing Excellence.* Walnut Creek, CA: Left Coast Press.

Smithsonian Institution. [2016]. *Museum on Main Street: Exhibition Planning Guide.* Washington, DC: Smithsonian Institution. PDF e-publication. Accessed September 1, 2020. https:// museumonmainstreet.org/resource/exhibition-planning-guide.

Trofanenko, Brenda, and Avner Segall, eds. 2014. *Beyond Pedagogy: Considering the Public Purpose of Museums.* Rotterdam: Sense Publishers.

Write It!

Text and Labels

ALTHOUGH SOME ITEMS ON VIEW are self-explanatory, most exhibited items need to be described to some degree so viewers recognize what they are looking at, and to understand how each piece fits into your larger narrative. Think of display items as characters in a play. The cast tells the story and your audience meets them one by one. So, too, with an exhibit. Each book or item holds a defined role that supports the overall production, and it is primarily through text, as with dialogue, that you tell your story.

Types of Text and Labels

Institutions of all types do not seem to agree on a universal lexicon to describe the written support materials accompanying exhibited items. Some refer to the information as *text*, others *labels*, some call it *copy* or a *script*, and other places refer to textual elements as *didactics* or simply as the *story*. There is a sea of terminology discussing the written components of exhibitions and displays, but in essence, collectively, these written parts serve to:

- Identify objects
- Convey interpretive information
- Explain an item's significance or history
- Engage viewers in reflection or appreciation
- Acknowledge exhibit supporters
- Help direct visitors through your exhibit

Advice on word counts come from studies primarily conducted in museums.[1] Your library setting may be different. Your audience's needs and preferences for text length can be higher or lower than the studied norms, and with trials and observation, you will get a feel for what is meaningful and satisfies your audience.

Common Types of Text and Labels

Introductory Panel

Generally, introductory panels are positioned at the beginning of an exhibit and tell the overall themes and aims of the exhibit and provide backstories and history about an era, time period, or place relevant to the exhibit. Often these panels are intentionally larger than other text panels elsewhere in the exhibit, and frequently these have the most text. Introductory panels can be as few as 50 words, but become overwhelming when they approach 150 words or surpass 200 words.

Case Panel

Curators use case panel text to provide information about the themes and sub-story of items in a particular case or grouping of items. Typically, case panels do not refer to specific materials. Case panels approaching 100 words or more than 150 words tend to be too long.

Sidebar or Section Panel

This supplementary text is used inside a case or near a grouping of items to provide second-tier interpretive information. The sidebar or section panel relays interesting facts or provides further information. Though not critical to the main message, these text panels dive a bit deeper into the subject and are often used sparingly to capture points curators want to share, somewhat as a bonus. Keep these panels short for impact—generally 50–100 words.

Item Label

Item labels identify individual items and describe materials on view. Text can be strictly bibliographic information (author, date, publisher, call number, etc.) or a combination of a bibliographic header with short interpretive informational text that calls attention to unique features or provides further explanations. Item labels are short captions and are most effective when they are under 50 words.

Tombstones

Sometimes people refer to labels that contain only bibliographic or general identification as *tombstones*. Also, some refer to the bibliographic item-identification information (author, date, publisher, call number, etc.) as the *tombstone*. You may decide to simply list main titles and forgo lengthy subtitles to streamline these identifiers.

Pull Quote

These labels highlight short excerpts, quotes, facts, or lists. Often, graphic design features help pull quote panels stand apart from other labels through the use of color, fonts, or spacing. Pull quotes are used to prompt reflection and help synthesize dense information that might be more intelligible in list form. Like sidebars, keep these short for impact. Typically a sentence or two, but if needed, a short passage will illustrate an important point.

Credit Panel or Donor Panel

These panels are used to publicly thank and acknowledge people and groups who participated in the creation of the exhibit. The panels are often placed off to the side at the start of the exhibit or at the exhibit's end. These panels do not help tell the story and are not explanatory, and they can be places to include branding marks and logos that promote your organization or supportive partners.

Wayfinding or Usage Labels

Directional signage can be used in exhibitions to help visitors navigate a space or explain how to use equipment or interactives. These explanatory labels are aids intended to support a positive visitor experience.

⑥ Content Development Best Practices

During your research and planning phase, explore your topic to gain expertise in the subject matter and get to know key issues, achievements, and highpoints about the area. Find fun personal accounts, inspiring facts, and small stories behind the big topic. As you investigate and dive into your subject, you are bound to learn fascinating information and widen your knowledge, but remember, the most effective exhibits are those that tell focused stories and do not overwhelm visitors. To help you streamline your narrative during the exhibition development phase, consider writing out a few big picture aims—such as the main idea and three key takeaways—that you feel are essential to communicate to visitors. If you are able to do this in a few sentences, chances are, you have a solid handle on your topic and have honed the particular angle you would like to share with visitors. It is helpful to write out your main idea and key messages and consult them frequently as you develop the exhibit. This exercise will help guide the items you select and how you describe them.

The Smithsonian Institution's exhibition development team works by creating an interpretive hierarchy during master planning phases.[2] At the top of their pyramid is the big idea, "the overarching message that visitors should understand upon leaving the exhibit." In the middle, are the key messages that support the big idea and "provide a conceptual framework that drives content development." At the base are critical questions "that the exhibit should answer for the visitors."[3] This model can be a helpful tool that guides your exhibit development work and keeps you focused to tell a well-thought-out story.

Layered Approach

Museum exhibition developers approach interpretive storytelling using a holistic approach referred to as *layering*.[4] Simply put, this strategy provides information through an assortment of modes, thought of as layers, such as text, interactives, videos, images, quotes, graphs, charts, and so on. These various layers help enliven the visitor experience, and they also speak to different learning modalities. Though this strategy helps ensure that exhibits are not too text dense and monotone, you should not feel obliged to insert AV materials, charts, or pull quotes into your exhibit if the nature of the show does not warrant these sorts of materials. Use them judiciously, but consider including them whenever appropriate.

Length

Overall, visitor studies have documented that people respond best to succinct labels.[5] Be brief, and straightforward with your writing. Long sentences can be off-putting and tend to deter reading. Break up lengthy sentences into parts. Studies have determined that the average person reads 250 words a minute standing in an exhibit setting.[6] Sentences shorter than 12–15 words with 130–150 syllables per 100 words are easy to read.[7] Also, mix up the length of sentences. Variety is energizing.

Verve Welcomed!

Engaging copy will hook readers. Write action sentences and, within your text, ask readers questions and prompt responses with commands. For example:

> Censorship has blurry edges. Should some information be restricted? Are some materials inappropriate for certain readers? Consider hate speech, bomb designs, personal records, misinformation, and pornography. Should these materials *always* be available? Questions like these are much of what makes censorship so hard to legislate, or even discuss. In this exhibit, explore how you personally feel about what is and is not acceptable.[8]

Punctuation

Punctuation can add spice, but watch not to overuse exclamation points, question marks, and dashes. For readability, try avoiding semicolons and break lengthy sentences apart. Though grammatically correct, readers may find multipart lines hard to follow. Consider using italics to offset foreign words, technical terms, or keywords readers may not know. Italics can add emphasis and highlight new information. Bolding titles sets them apart and adds emphasis, but within the body of text, it is not as effective as italics to highlight or provide emphasis. Underlining text is clunky and sort of "screamy." Avoid using all caps for similar reasons.

Reading Level

For a general museum audience, writers often aim for text at a sixth-grade reading level.[9] Your institution may be engaging a different audience, or a particular exhibit or display will target a select group of viewers. These standards are nice guideposts to consider, but speak to your audience. Online tools such as Readable help you analyze and evaluate reading levels.

Tone

As you consider tone, remember, exhibits should be fun and not something visitors need to trudge through, and text should not make them feel talked down to. Let your copy be informative but not pedantic. Find your institutional voice (or voice for each exhibit) and adjust your tone to engage your audience. Be welcoming and approachable.

Veracity

Your audience expects reliable, correct information. As you develop your exhibit, research and fact-check extensively. Subject experts may visit and point out embarrassing errors, or worse, incorrect information could spread.

It is important to produce clean, error-free text. When authoring text, you may overlook spelling errors and typos. It is very helpful to enlist others to proofread your work. Some editors ask multiple people to read copy, some read text out loud or use computer text readers to listen to it aloud, and some begin proofing with their last pages where errors have a way of slipping past tired readers. Be scrupulous on your acknowledgment and donor panels. Triple check the spelling of personal names and remain mindful of people's preferences for nicknames, middle initials, and honorifics.

☺ Style Guides

Presenting clean, error-free text that conforms to standard word usage helps you present labels that are correct, easy to read, and do not distract visitors. Viewers, knowingly or not, appreciate consistency and accuracy, and evenness promotes readability and avoids distractions that inhibit comprehension.

Style guides set standards for writing, formatting, punctuation, abbreviations, and a host of presentation options and help your writing be consistent and easy to read. *The Chicago Manual of Style* describes itself as "the indispensable reference for writers, editors, proofreaders, indexers, copywriters, designers, and publishers, informing the editorial canon with sound, definitive advice."[10] Many label writers adopt *The Chicago Manual of Style* (or another published style manual) to resolve specific grammatical, word usage, and stylistic questions.

With exhibition writing, you will tackle site-specific information such as how to abbreviate your institution's name. In print, is it The University of Delaware Library, the University of Delaware Library, or University of Delaware Library? That is, is the name without the definitive article, and if included, is it capitalized or lower case? All are grammatically correct, but being consistent in your usage polishes your presentation and provides readers with consistency that demonstrates reliability and thoroughness, which strengthens your work and adds credibility.

Your style guide can help provide you with advice that goes beyond grammar conventions. Exhibition label writing often presents you with situations where you need to carefully consider subtle messages. For instance, it is correct to list dates as BC (before Christ) and BCE (before the common era), but as an organization, is one more appropriate for your audience? As you encounter options such as these and take time to consider wider implications, you can document decisions and establish your house standard in your library's exhibit style guide.

In-house style guides are not static and will evolve over time as you encounter particular situations and wrestle to sensible conclusions, informed by visitor study observations and house policies. As a reference tool, style guides help your textual output remain consistent within an exhibit and across time in other exhibits.

Design Tips and Visual Presentation Standards

There is not a definitive source for visual presentation standards and conventions in exhibition work. Organizations generally develop their own exhibition label conventions based on user experience information and other scientific data. As libraries adopt standards, they typically document and codify them in their house style guides. Beyond improving accuracy and consistency, style guides can expand to document best practices for label design. User study data provides insight into visitor preferences for sizes, fonts, and colors that help audiences consume label information with ease.

If you are a librarian with graphic design skills, exhibits will be your time to shine. If you do not have art and visual communication training, fear not. With attention to detail, seeking out informal training, and following best practices advice, your presentations can be effective and support a positive visitor experience. If you are new to graphic design and typography, experiment and enlist support to guide your work and provide you with constructive feedback.

Components of Legibility

When considering presentation, legibility should drive your production. Leading museum label research expert Beverly Serrell identifies the following as key factors determining legibility: font familiarity, type size, letter spacing, word spacing, line spacing, reading distance, and color combinations.[11]

Fonts

Familiar fonts, such as Times New Roman, Helvetica, and Arial, are widely used and readers' eyes track them with ease in part because they are accustomed to seeing these styles.[12] As a rule of thumb, fonts that run "tall" with a pitched vertical component and tight letter spacing, as well as fonts that run "short" with wider letters and spacing, are more difficult for people to read.[13] Selecting a familiar font may seem boring, but as a safe choice, it gets the job done. Both serif and sans serif fonts can be easily recognizable (see figures 4.1 and 4.2).[14]

More advanced graphic designers will select from a wider collection of fonts to match the tone of the exhibit, and perhaps mix serif and sans serif fonts between headers and body text.

Times New Roman

Southwestern Silver

The southwestern culture region is centered in Arizona and New Mexico. Its main inhabitants, the *Navajo* and *Pueblo*, learned the art of silver smithing from their Mexican neighbors in the 1850s.

Compare with "shorter" Baskerville Old Face serif font:

Baskerville Old Face

Southwestern Silver

The southwestern culture region is centered in Arizona and New Mexico. Its main inhabitants, the *Navajo* and *Pueblo*, learned the art of silver smithing from their Mexican neighbors in the 1850s.

Figure 4.1. Comparing legibility of serif fonts. Notice how the taller sample on top is easier to read. *Patti Gibbons.*

Ariel

Southwestern Silver

The southwestern culture region is centered in Arizona and New Mexico. Its main inhabitants, the *Navajo* and *Pueblo*, learned the art of silver smithing from their Mexican neighbors in the 1850s.

Compare with "slender" Ariel Narrow san serif font:

Ariel Narrow

Southwestern Silver

The southwestern culture region is centered in Arizona and New Mexico. Its main inhabitants, the *Navajo* and *Pueblo*, learned the art of silver smithing from their Mexican neighbors in the 1850s.

Figure 4.2. Comparing legibility of sans serif fonts. Notice how the wider sample on top is easier to read. *Patti Gibbons.*

Sizes

Most readers standing twenty inches away from panels can comfortably read 18-point text.[15] As a general rule of thumb, this is a good size for body text passages. With captions and headers, consider increasing the font size to add emphasis, using 20–24-point sizes.[16] With bigger introductory panels, larger text helps increase readability and distinguish this area as the exhibit's starting point. Lettering 28–48 points in size is effective; larger than 48 points becomes hard for one's eye to track.[17]

Spacing

Spacing between letters, between words, and between lines influences readability. Experienced graphic designers and typographers will expertly finesse these spacing points, but as a guide for those new to design, err toward established standards (such as your software's default set points).

In general, visitors can read lines that are 50–65 characters per line with ease. If you are placing text on wide panels, consider using two columns of text that are each about this length. Visitor studies show that more than two columns becomes difficult to read, and visually creates a text-dense block that is off-putting.[18]

Additionally, studies show that left-justified text with a natural "ragged" right end is easiest for a reader's eyes to track (see figure 4.3).[19] When using ragged right text, some layout designers prune and manipulate line breaks to avoid widows, and shape paragraphs to form tapering right edge curves. Other graphic designers justify text and prefer defined

Styles

Early jewelry was plain and heavy, but southwestern smiths soon

created lighter, more elaborate styles. These fancier designs

appealed to travelers' tastes. In the 1880s, Navajo makers began

adding eye-catching turquoise and stamped more designs onto the

jewelry. Can you tell which pieces are the oldest?

Styles

Early jewelry was plain and heavy, but southwestern smiths

soon created lighter, more elaborate styles. These fancier designs

appealed to travelers' tastes. In the 1880s, Navajo makers began

adding eye-catching turquoise and stamped more designs onto

the jewelry. Can you tell which pieces are the oldest?

Figure 4.3. Manipulating line spacing so a paragraph's right edge curves like a hill helps guide a reader's eyes through the text. *Patti Gibbons.*

left and right edges that produce a very crisp look, but could include gaps and tight spots depending on how word and character counts land.

Colors

In general, exhibits benefit from color, and your panels and labels do not need to be black and white. Consider using colored backgrounds and lighter text, or dark colored text on lighter backgrounds to create a pleasant aesthetic experience. The key is to provide a sharp enough contrast so letters pop and are easy to read. Color can help you reinforce or tie into exhibit themes. For instance, if your exhibit covers topics about nature, perhaps verdant greens would be an apt choice that echoes your subtle messages. Online tools such as WebAIM's Contrast Checker and Coblis Color Blind Simulator help you identify problematic color combinations.

Color can also help you distinguish thematic sections and guide visitor flow through the space. You may want to divide your exhibit into chronological timeframes. Using color schemes—harmonious (colors adjacent on the color wheel) or triadic (colors formed from equally distant colors on the wheel), you can designate colors to each grouping to help reinforce your timeline and separate the groupings: Early Printing (blue), Renaissance Printing (red), and Modern Printing (yellow). Beyond color categories, some designers employ icons or branding marks to designate labels in particular sections. This can be effective if subtle, or it can be distracting if not done well.

 **Examples**

Introductory Panel

165 words

Trinkets or Treasures? Rethinking Southwestern Tourist Jewelry

Until the turn of the twentieth century, indigenous people from the American Southwest crafted for themselves traditional jewelry as decoration or symbols of wealth. In 1899, Navajo and Pueblo craftsmen began producing bracelets, necklaces, and earrings for commercial trade. Bustling train lines and Route 66 traffic brought a steady stream of vacationers to the area and visitors purchased souvenir jewelry, along with other keepsakes. A new trade blossomed.

Often dismissed as lesser art forms, today's historians and jewelry connoisseurs are rethinking the indigenous trade jewelry produced in the Southwest during the early twentieth century. Examining the characteristic design, smithing, and lapidary stonework, specialists point to a refined tradition and body of work that surpasses mere tourist-grade craft. Many pieces are distinctive and hold the hallmarks of an artisan tradition unique to the region.

The books and objects on view show the range of jewelry, exemplify styles, and demonstrate the look of jewelry typical of the Southwest from 1900 to 1950.

Case Panel

88 words

Southwestern Silver

The Southwestern culture region is centered in Arizona and New Mexico. Its main inhabitants, the *Navajo* and *Pueblo*, learned the art of silversmithing from their Mexican neighbors in the 1850s.

Nineteenth-century Southwestern artists used iron tools to pound small pieces of silver into different shapes. Later artists learned to melt silver and pour the hot liquid into handmade casts. Similar to ice cube trays, casts reshape liquids while they cool into solids. Once hardened, artists file, carve, and stamp designs onto the newly formed silver.

Sidebar or Section Panel

47 words

Styles

Early jewelry was plain and heavy, but Southwestern smiths soon created lighter, more elaborate styles. These fancier designs appealed to travelers' tastes. In the 1880s, Navajo makers began adding eye-catching turquoise and stamped more designs onto the jewelry. Can you tell which pieces are the oldest?

Item Label

55 words

Indian Silver: Navajo and Pueblo Jewelers

Margery Bedinger
Albuquerque: University of New Mexico Press, 1973

Take a close look at the jewelry. Notice the moons, stars, crosses, and flowers. What do these patterns represent to you? Southwestern artists borrowed designs from other cultures and used them decoratively. These crosses are not vested with religious meanings.

Tombstone

15 words

Indian Silver: Navajo and Pueblo Jewelers

Margery Bedinger
Albuquerque: University of New Mexico Press, 1973

Pull Quote

55 words

When I was eight years old, my mother surprised me with a silver squash blossom necklace she purchased at a roadside stand during our family trip through New Mexico. The jeweler told her the silver beads could ward off illness, and throughout childhood, I would wear it at the first sign of sickness.

—JANE DOE

◎ Definitions

- Font—a set of printing typeface that is a consistent style throughout its character run
- Layered content development—a strategy employed by exhibit content developers to provide exhibition information and interpretations using a range of methods (thought of as layers), such as text, interactive components, quotes, charts, and other graphics
- Style guide—a reference manual prescribing accepted or adopted styles in punctuation, formatting, and grammar, and that, with exhibition guides, can document visual conventions and best practices

ⓖ Key Points

- You will develop a variety of written support materials to accompany and explain the exhibited items
- Text and labels are most effective when succinct, engaging, and in a tone crafted for a particular audience
- Style guides help you standardize written and visual presentations and can be customized by your institution
- Graphic design and typography enhance how you convey your story, and there is an art behind the science of best practices for visual presentation in exhibitions

ⓖ Notes

1. Serrell, Beverly. 2015. *Exhibition Labels: An Interpretive Approach.* Lanham, MD: Rowman & Littlefield, 97.

2. Smithsonian Exhibits. 2018. *A Guide to Exhibit Development.* Landover, MD: Smithsonian Exhibits, 6–7.

3. Smithsonian Exhibits. 2018. *A Guide to Exhibit Development.* Landover, MD: Smithsonian Exhibits, 7.

4. Serrell, Beverly. 2015. *Exhibition Labels: An Interpretive Approach.* Lanham, MD: Rowman & Littlefield, 156–59.

5. Lord, Barry, and Gail Dexter Lord, eds. 2002. *The Manual of Museum Exhibitions.* Walnut Creek, CA: AltaMira Press, 140.

6. Serrell, Beverly. 2015. *Exhibition Labels: An Interpretive Approach.* Lanham, MD: Rowman & Littlefield, 97.

7. Serrell, Beverly. 2015. *Exhibition Labels: An Interpretive Approach.* Lanham, MD: Rowman & Littlefield, 284.

8. Palmer, Ada. 2018. *Censorship and Information Control.* September 17, 2018–December 14, 2018. Special Collections Research Center, University of Chicago Library, Chicago.

9. Serrell, Beverly. 2015. *Exhibition Labels: An Interpretive Approach.* Lanham, MD: Rowman & Littlefield, 87.

10. University of Chicago Press. *The Chicago Manual of Style Online.* 17th edition. Accessed September 1, 2020. https://www.chicagomanualofstyle.org/home.html.

11. Serrell, Beverly. 2015. *Exhibition Labels: An Interpretive Approach.* Lanham, MD: Rowman & Littlefield, 267–70.

12. Serrell, Beverly. 2015. *Exhibition Labels: An Interpretive Approach.* Lanham, MD: Rowman & Littlefield, 269.

13. Serrell, Beverly. 2015. *Exhibition Labels: An Interpretive Approach.* Lanham, MD: Rowman & Littlefield, 271.

14. Serrell, Beverly. 2015. *Exhibition Labels: An Interpretive Approach.* Lanham, MD: Rowman & Littlefield, 270–71.

15. Serrell, Beverly. 2015. *Exhibition Labels: An Interpretive Approach.* Lanham, MD: Rowman & Littlefield, 275.

16. Serrell, Beverly. 2015. *Exhibition Labels: An Interpretive Approach.* Lanham, MD: Rowman & Littlefield, 275.

17. Serrell, Beverly. 2015. *Exhibition Labels: An Interpretive Approach.* Lanham, MD: Rowman & Littlefield, 275–76.

18. Serrell, Beverly. 2015. *Exhibition Labels: An Interpretive Approach.* Lanham, MD: Rowman & Littlefield, 279.

19. Serrell, Beverly. 2015. *Exhibition Labels: An Interpretive Approach.* Lanham, MD: Rowman & Littlefield, 276.

References

Lord, Barry, and Gail Dexter Lord, eds. 2002. *The Manual of Museum Exhibitions.* Walnut Creek, CA: AltaMira Press.

Palmer, Ada. 2018. *Censorship and Information Control.* September 17, 2018–December 14, 2018. Special Collections Research Center, University of Chicago Library, Chicago.

Serrell, Beverly. 2015. *Exhibition Labels: An Interpretive Approach.* Lanham, MD: Rowman & Littlefield.

Smithsonian Exhibits. 2018. *A Guide to Exhibit Development.* Landover, MD: Smithsonian Exhibits.

University of Chicago Press. 2017. *The Chicago Manual of Style Online.* 17th ed. Accessed September 1, 2020. https://www.chicagomanualofstyle.org/home.html.

Resources Mentioned in This Chapter

Coblis Color Blindness Simulator: https://www.color-blindness.com/coblis-color-blindness-simulator/

Readable: https://app.readable.com/text/

WebAIM Contrast Checker: https://webaim.org/resources/contrastchecker/

Further Reading

Falk, John H., and Lynn D. Dierking. 2018. *Learning from Museums.* Lanham, MD: Rowman & Littlefield.

Mason, Rhiannon, Alistair Robinson, and Emma Coffield. 2018. *Museum and Gallery Studies: The Basics.* New York: Routledge.

Perry, Deborah L. 2012. *What Makes Learning Fun? Principles for the Design of Intrinsically Motivating Museum Exhibits.* Lanham, MD: AltaMira Press.

Stringer, Katie. 2014. *Programming for People with Special Needs: A Guide for Museums and Historic Sites.* Lanham, MD: Rowman & Littlefield.

Wallace, Margot. 2014. *Writing for Museums.* Lanham, MD: Rowman & Littlefield.

Wells, Marcella, Barbara Butler, and Judith Koke. 2013. *Interpretive Planning for Museums: Integrating Visitor Perspectives in Decision Making.* Walnut Creek, CA: Left Coast Press.

Build It!

Physical Exhibits and Displays

THE EXHIBIT PRODUCTION PHASE is a transformative time when you begin seeing your ideas come to life. In three dimensions, and often with multisensory aspects, your story starts to take shape as you get ready for visitors. The following are best practice recommendations, guidelines, and pro tips that will help protect materials, make installations run smoothly, and help improve the overall look and feel of your physical exhibits and displays.

Conservation and Collection Care Considerations

Exhibition display can physically strain library materials. During exhibits, books and archival items are mounted, strapped, and matted, and are subjected to environmental factors that can be harmful to an item's long-term physical preservation. Despite exposure to risk and wear, conservators who specialize in the preservation and treatment of cultural heritage materials agree that most library resources can be safely exhibited for periods of about three to four months.[1] To minimize potential damage, conservators outline specific recommendations for the display of delicate and sensitive materials. These professional best practice guidelines are especially important for rare, fragile, or unique items, but may not be critical to circulating collections.

Exhibit-related collection care best practice addresses:

- Lighting
- Temperature and relative humidity
- Handling
- Mounts
- Materials
- Security
- Disaster response preparation

Lighting

Sensitive library resources such as hand-colored historic prints, color photographs, newspapers, just to name a few, can be damaged by sunlight, UV light, and light intensity. Conservators recommend using non-UV emitting lighting in exhibit spaces—such as LED, incandescent bulbs, or fluorescent bulbs outfitted with UV filtering sleeves—and avoiding displaying sensitive items in areas that receive direct sunlight.[2] Light level output can be measured with light meters and the following are recommended levels for sensitive materials:[3]

- Highly sensitive materials (hand-colored prints, watercolors, textiles): 5 foot candles/ 50 lux
- Moderately sensitive materials (black-and-white photographs, archival documents): 10 foot candles/100 lux
- Slightly light-sensitive materials (black ink printing, paintings): 35 foot candles/ 350 lux

Rare book libraries test light levels during installation and spot test throughout the run of an exhibit. Additionally, dataloggers and analog monitoring devices, such as blue wool scales, can be placed near items to measure and quantify light exposure.

Temperature and Relative Humidity

Ideal temperatures for sensitive, cultural heritage materials often are cooler than visitors may tolerate or find comfortable. Many rare book libraries compromise standards and allow their gallery temperatures to be warmer than long-term storage rooms that aim to provide optimal environments. For short-term exposures such as exhibition periods, temperatures of 68–72°F (20–22°C) are generally accepted.[4]

Controlling humidity in a library space is challenging, and not all library mechanical systems provide humidity control. Rare book venues tend to be the types of libraries investing in expensive mechanical systems. For most paper-based library materials, conservators recommend relative humidity levels set between 45 and 55 percent.[5] With both temperature and relative humidity, it is very important that levels remain as consistent as possible, with slow changes. Ideally, it is best for the materials if temperatures do not change more than 5°F or relative humidity levels fluctuate +/–5 percent within a twenty-four-hour period.[6]

Handling

Careful handling prevents accidents and damage. Extra care is needed during exhibit phases when materials are mounted and awaiting display or being removed from view at the end of a show. Work slowly, and observe the condition of items throughout the exhibit setup and takedown process. If you notice a physical flaw or trouble spot, be certain to monitor weak spots and stop immediately if conditions worsen.

Conservators generally recommend that people handle most library materials with clean hands rather than gloved hands in order to provide staff with the most dexterity and tactile sensitivity.[7] Gloves can be bulky and inhibit safe handling, especially when turning book pages. There are a few exceptions, such as when handling photographs, metal items, and ivory. Wearing gloves when working with those items help prevent you from transferring hand oils that damage the surfaces of these sensitive materials. Both cotton and neoprene gloves are effective.

Installation and deinstallation times are ripe for accidents. Before handling materials, know where you are moving them to and plan safe ways to pick up and transport items. Old books with loose covers could easily break, but holding them gently with two hands and supporting weak areas will help lessen the likelihood of damage.

Mounts

Book mounts are supportive devices that cradle a book during display and alleviate pressures that could damage its structure. Book mounts can be purchased from specialty suppliers or created in-house. "Off the rack" products from archival suppliers may provide approximate fits, while custom-made mounts are fabricated to a book's precise dimensions and page opening. When positioned in a mount, a book's text block is secured and pages immobilized with archival Mylar straps that do not obscure the materials from the viewer (see figures 5.1 and 5.2).

Figure 5.1. Mounts supporting books on display. *Patti Gibbons.*

Figure 5.2. Mounts supporting books on display. *Patti Gibbons.*

Flat items such as letters, photos, and charts require mounting devices for exhibitions. These items can be matted and framed, simply matted, or mounted to archival board with clear photo corners or small magnets. Flat mounts need to aptly protect the materials they display and not cause harm. Conservators at your library, trained exhibition staff, or freelance mount makers can make an array of custom mounts.

Materials

Mounting apparatus used inside cases needs to be selected with care, and with rare and sensitive items, it needs to be made from archival-quality stock that will not harm library materials. Conservators have tested a range of exhibition supplies and recommend lignin-free, acid-free mat board, and inert Mylar straps and photo corners.[8] In general, avoid glues, tapes, wood, or office-grade supplies when working with rare and unique library items. Consult with a conservator if you have questions about materials. Similarly, materials used to construct cases that house artifacts need to be chemically inert and not off-gas and harm materials.[9]

Security

Displays and exhibits require levels of security appropriate to your library setting. Rare book and archival libraries generally uphold the highest security protocols and only display items inside locking cases with smash-resistant vitrine tops and, additionally, are likely to protect materials with an integrated electronic alarm system, security cameras, and perhaps guards.

With circulating collections, libraries may not need as many layers of security, and aims for general collections may focus on ways to deter people from handling, touching, or disturbing displays and exhibits. This can be done by putting books inside cases, on stands, or behind roped areas, depending on your security needs and your exhibition design choices.

Disaster Response Preparation

If your institution has a formal disaster response plan for collection items, consider the special needs of exhibited materials. You may develop separate procedures to track and protect these items, and any loaned materials will likely involve proactive attention and planning.[10]

Project Management During Exhibit Development

Great planning makes for a smooth exhibition experience, and there are many details to tend to and decisions to make that impact the process. For each exhibit project, you will develop a schedule that defines key milestones and dates for deliverables. Some exhibit developers find it helpful to use project management software, such as Gantt charts (seen in figure 5.3), to track concurrent deadlines. Identifying systems that work for you and your organization can help you stay organized and on schedule.

Design and Production

During your project development phases, you will identify and address the design and production tasks for your exhibit. Exhibit design work covers everything from establishing the look and aesthetic of your components, to selecting typography and color, as well as determining item placement and the arrangement of cases. An art or design background is certainly helpful when working on these tasks, but careful studying of your space and visitors can help you achieve effective and pleasing results.

Design

Floor Layout

When planning your exhibit, confirm exactly where it will be located. Some libraries have dedicated gallery space, others have informal areas for displays. When you have selected and scheduled the space, you can begin planning the order and flow of your cases, components, and materials. Some exhibit designers use CAD 3-D software programs such as SketchUp or Vectorworks to design schematic floor plans. Some people simply sketch arrangements of the space on paper. Perhaps crude, but in some situations, that is all the formality needed to effectively plan case placement. During this phase, determine the placement of all cases and stands, informed by the order you would like your visitors to move through the exhibit. (See figure 5.4.)

Exhibition Planning

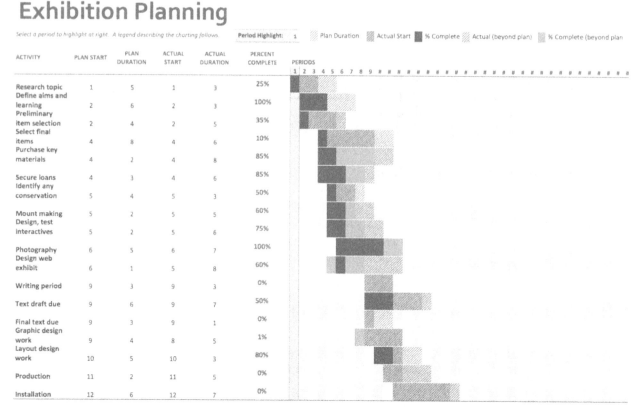

ACTIVITY	PLAN START	PLAN DURATION	ACTUAL START	ACTUAL DURATION	PERCENT COMPLETE
Research topic	1	5	1	3	25%
Define aims and learning	2	6	2	3	100%
Preliminary item selection	2	4	2	5	35%
Select final items	4	8	4	6	10%
Purchase key materials	4	2	4	8	85%
Secure loans	4	3	4	6	85%
Identify any conservation	5	4	5	3	50%
Mount making	5	2	5	5	60%
Design, test interactives	5	2	5	6	75%
Photography	6	5	6	7	100%
Design web exhibit	6	1	5	8	60%
Writing period	9	3	9	3	0%
Text draft due	9	6	9	7	50%
Final text due	9	3	9	1	0%
Graphic design work	9	4	8	5	1%
Layout design work	10	5	10	3	80%
Production	11	2	11	5	0%
Installation	12	6	12	7	0%

Figure 5.3. Sample Gantt chart detailing exhibition development phases and tasks. *Patti Gibbons.*

Be sure to consider general accessibility issues during the planning phases, leaving clear space around components at a minimum of 30 by 48 in. (76 x 122 cm)[11] and wider—especially if you foresee heavy stroller traffic or visits by wheelchair users. If you are including interactive equipment that requires electricity or data lines, be sure to consider their placement adjacent to utility portals. Work to identify and eliminate trip hazards.

If your facility allows, including space for seating is an often-overlooked amenity that visitors enjoy. Having a place to sit or talk as a group makes the exhibition experience more pleasant and encourages people to stay longer.

Item Placement

For each case or display area, you need to determine how to position and group individual items, along with accompanying text, labels, and any graphic elements. For visual variety, work away from static placement and monotonous rows. Vary placement. Use risers to lift items. Position harder to reach items closer to the viewer.

Some designers explore placement options virtually and simulate potential layouts in CAD programs. Others find it helpful to work directly with the materials and organize them in mock-ups before the exhibit installation. They may achieve this by creating templates of the case or space layout, and then moving items around on top of the templates. Your item configuration work informs your mount making and label creation, and by working in advance on placement, you can build mounts that lift and tilt to provide visitors with optimal views, and you are able to position labels that complement items and make it easy for viewers to connect. (See figure 5.5.)

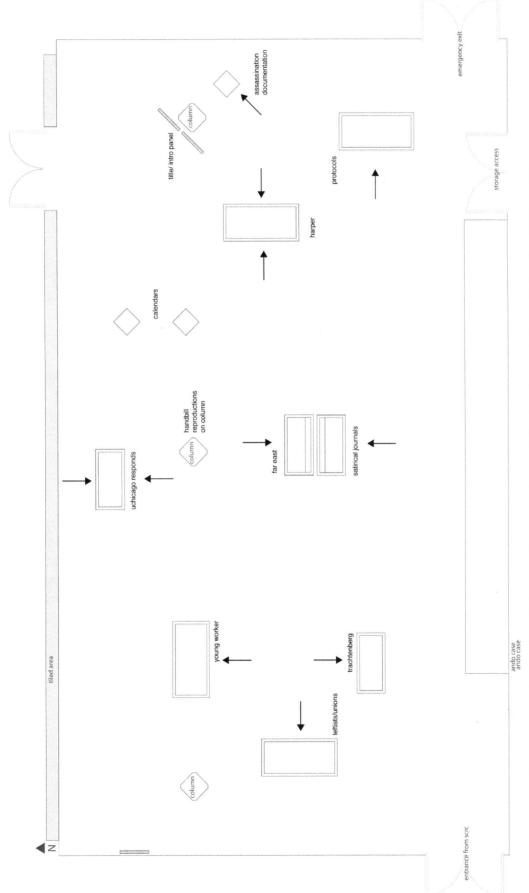

Figure 5.4. Sample floor elevation drawing for exhibit case placement. *Special Collections Research Center, University of Chicago Library.*

When standing, adults can comfortably see materials at heights of 43–67 in. (109–170 cm).[12] Eye-level range for adults seated in wheelchairs and children (ages 8–12) standing is 40–52 in. (102–132 cm).[13] The Smithsonian Institution's accessibility guidelines recommend that floor cases and exhibit barriers have a maximum height of 36 in. (92 cm).[14] When exhibiting materials in cases and on walls, keep materials and text panels within these sightlines. For hanging artwork, most museums and galleries follow a universal standard and position items so the center of the work is 58 in. (147 cm) above the ground.[15]

Graphics

During your design phase, you will develop a range of graphic components. Visitors respond to images, and including eye-catching posters and enlarged images entices and encourages people to explore and helps enliven and enrich your exhibit. Additionally, you will create visually appealing labels, text panels, and signage that take graphic design principles into account. (*See chapter 4 for guidance on text production.*) You can hire designers to tackle these jobs if needed.

Production

After your detailed design work is finished, you switch gears and begin fabricating or ordering the physical elements required for the exhibit, such as mounts, mats, frames, labels, text panels, posters, risers, sign stands, audiovisual components, and more. These elements can be made in-house, by colleagues elsewhere in your library, or by freelancers. Some materials can be reused in future exhibits.

Mounts for Books and Flat Items

Many exhibit librarians make book mounts and mats for flat items such as letters and newspapers using archival mat board, Vivak, or Plexiglas (see figures 5.6 and 5.7). All mounts need to safely present materials on view and many can be challenging to make, but you can learn techniques through classes, online resources, and repetitive practice. Perfect fit with full support is essential when working with rare, unique, and delicate materials. Libraries with rare holdings generally have trained staff to design and fabricate appropriate mounts, but if not, it is critical to enlist proper help to fabricate mounts—and to also appeal to the library's administration to build professional expertise on staff or allocate an appropriate budget to care for these important materials during display.

In-House Label Production

With relatively few supplies and simple equipment, libraries of all sizes and types can make attractive exhibition labels and panels. Using graphic design software, such as Adobe Creative Suite, you can lay out labels that you print and mount in-house.

During your design work, experiment with fonts and text colors. Try backgrounds and light text, or dark-colored text on a lighter background. Color adds interest and has a more professional, polished look than basic black-and-white printing.

Labels can be printed on paper and then mounted to stiff foam core boards or thin, rigid mat board using a double-stick transfer adhesive known as PMA (positionable

Section 12 - University of Chicago Responds

Side 1

1. Dust jacket Lyford P. Edwards, *The Natural History of Revolutions*, 1927
2. Typescript "How Revolutions Begin"
3. Document: Chauncy D. Harris' work founding the U of C's Slavic Department
   1 orginal document over 2 facsimiles
4. Proposal to Ford Foundation, 1960
5. Directory of Committee on Slavic Area Studies, 1964
6. Masaryk, Světová revoluce [World Revolution]. 1925

Side 2

6. DOC film poster: "Three Russian Directors" handbill
7. Photograph of Mary Seton
8. DOC film poster: *The General Line*
9. DOC film lecture notes for *The General Line*
10. DOC films poster - *Tsar to Lenin*
11. Doc Films posters - *Childhood of Maxim Gorki*

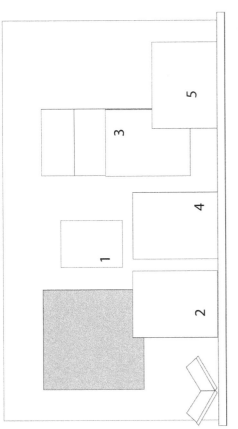

Side 1

Side 2

Figure 5.5.   Sample case elevation drawing for item placement. *Special Collections Research Center, University of Chicago Library.*

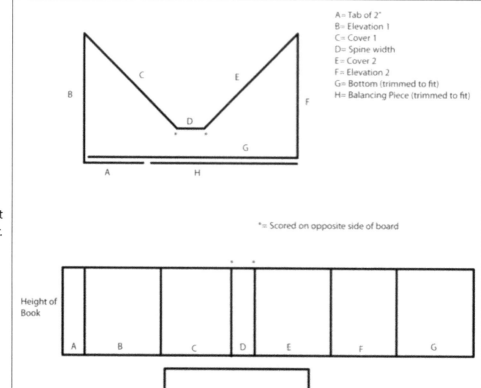

Figure 5.6. Book mount instructions. *Nadja Otikor.*

A= Tab of 2"
B= Elevation 1
C= Cover 1
D= Spine width
E= Cover 2
F= Elevation 2
G= Bottom (trimmed to fit)
H= Balancing Piece (trimmed to fit)

*= Scored on opposite side of board

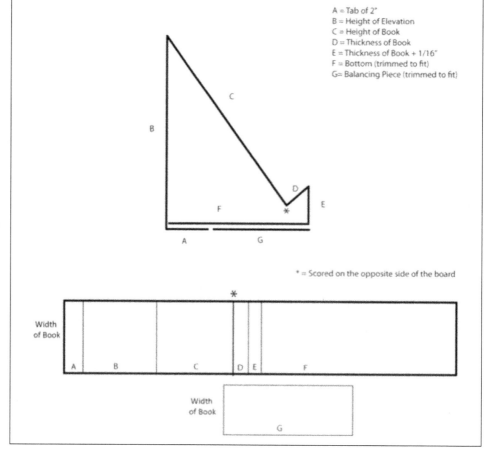

Figure 5.7. Upright book mount instructions. *Nadja Otikor.*

A = Tab of 2"
B = Height of Elevation
C = Height of Book
D = Thickness of Book
E = Thickness of Book + 1/16"
F = Bottom (trimmed to fit)
G= Balancing Piece (trimmed to fit)

*= Scored on the opposite side of the board

Figure 5.8. Board shear, tool used to cut large sheets of mat board. *Patti Gibbons.*

mounting adhesive) or slightly messier adhesive sprays, glues, or tapes. Mounting paper to board creates a rigid surface and these labels generally are durable enough for temporary exhibits. You can cut mat board using utility knives or craft scalpels and a ruler. If you have an opportunity to invest in larger equipment, a board shear can accommodate large sheets of mat board and make your work neater and quicker (see figure 5.8). Be exacting when producing mounted labels, panels, or signage of any kind. Work carefully and discard any imperfect items. Visitors will notice flawed work.

Retail copy centers can be an affordable graphic production resource. Most have design, print, and mounting services that can be helpful if you are not able to make items in-house.

In-House Graphic Production

A large range of graphic panels, oversized signs, banners, and other graphic elements can be produced in-house using high-quality printers. If you have access to a large-format printer, you can self-produce oversized graphic elements (up to around 48 inches wide by up to 80 feet long) on rolled paper media that you can hang or mount (see figure 5.9). Some retail copy centers can also help design, print, and mount large graphic panels such as main exhibit posters and banners.

Overall, exhibit component fabrication can happen in-house or be outsourced depending on staff expertise, budget, and equipment. Wherever you start, you can learn tricks and techniques, attend workshops, and develop production skills over time to increase your production portfolio. Build slowly and steadily. If you have an interest in learning more, aim to try new techniques each exhibit. Budget time in your production schedule for experimentation and learning.

Figure 5.9. Large-format printer used to create oversized exhibition graphics. *Patti Gibbons.*

Installation/Deinstallation and Maintenance

Installation

Installation is the time period when you set up materials in the exhibit. To best ensure that everything runs smoothly, and that materials are safely moved and accounted for throughout the process, it is essential to develop a detailed work plan before you begin. The work schedule should define roles, enumerate tasks, and map out the sequencing of duties.

For object security, the display area should be closed or roped off during the installation period and limit foot traffic to the exhibition team involved in the setup work to prevent accidents that could happen more easily when items are spread out awaiting installation. This is a crucial precaution with loans, and often explicitly required in the contract or terms of the loan agreement.

Dedicated workspace can be hard to find during the installation, and it is helpful to have a worktop surface like a portable table or wide cart on hand. This provides you with an improvised workspace throughout the installation. It is also helpful to create a tool and supply cart that you can bring to the space that has handy items you may need, such as hand tools, notepads, clipboards, scissors, measuring tapes, hand levels, extra book straps, conservation hand tools, and so forth. You can build your kit over time, adding items you identify as useful during your exhibit work.

Deinstallation

In comparison to the fussy, exacting installation period, work during deinstallation generally runs much faster, but still needs to be done with exacting care and advanced planning. Be sure to review any notes from the installation, especially on item condition, and setup, packing, or post-exhibit routing notes. Create a detailed schedule that identifies all tasks, the sequencing of duties, and the people assigned to execute each. Just as in the installation period, it is important to secure the space and limit traffic to essential project staff. Your tool kit and portable work surfaces will come in handy again.

Maintenance

To help ensure that materials are properly displayed, secured, and looking their best throughout the run of an exhibition, you need to monitor and maintain your exhibit spaces regularly. Maintenance checks involve cleaning exhibit cases and components to remove dust and smudges. Although not a glamorous task, it can provide you with insight into what cases are the most popular with visitors. If you find forehead prints frequently in the same spot, this might be an indicator that the item or label placement is difficult for visitors to see. Maintenance also involves checking and removing trash, sweeping/vacuuming floors, stocking takeaway stands, tidying interactive areas, and changing burned-out bulbs. High traffic areas will likely need more maintenance attention than areas visited less frequently. Some exhibits can afford weekly maintenance routines and attention before and after special events; others may need twice daily maintenance. Adjust your maintenance schedule to meet the needs of your program and space.

Monitoring

For object safety, you need to monitor your exhibit regularly. Routinely inspect items to ensure that everything is present. Check to see if any items or labels slipped. Look at item mounts. Do any show signs of distress? Look for graffiti in the exhibit area. Also, for environmental safety—especially of rare and fragile materials—set up a schedule to check temperature, humidity, and lighting levels. As you monitor, promptly address any issues you discover. Much as with your maintenance schedule, monitoring frequency is set by your particular venue's needs.

⊚ Definitions

- Conservator—professional trained to assess and treat cultural heritage materials in order to prolong their useful life span
- Gantt chart—complex bar chart / project management tool that tracks scheduling components across time and whose layout allows for easy comparison of timeline tasks
- PMA—positionable mounting adhesive sold in rolls or sheets; a transfer adhesive that can be rubbed/burnished onto the back side of papers to mount onto board for display

Key Points

- Preservation professionals have outlined best practices to minimize strain on materials during displays. The degree of preventative preservation steps is driven by the needs of items displayed.
- Mounts, mats, and other display apparatus are used to improve the viewing experience and minimize physical wear on items during exhibits. Rare, unique, and sensitive materials have more mounting-exacting requirements than circulating items.
- Meticulous project planning helps identify production needs and ensures a smoother exhibition experience
- Graphic design work and physical exhibition production work can be done by exhibit staff, colleagues in your library, or by freelance professionals. Mounts and reusable exhibit equipment can be custom-made or purchased from specialty vendors.

Notes

1. Northeast Document Conservation Center. 1999. "2.5 Protecting Paper and Book Collections during Exhibition." Accessed September 1, 2020. https://www.nedcc.org/free-resources/preservation-leaflets/2.-the-environment/2.5-protecting-paper-and-book-collections-during-exhibition.

2. Northeast Document Conservation Center. 1999. "2.5 Protecting Paper and Book Collections during Exhibition." Accessed September 1, 2020. https://www.nedcc.org/free-resources/preservation-leaflets/2.-the-environment/2.5-protecting-paper-and-book-collections-during-exhibition.

3. Lord, Barry, and Gail Dexter Lord, eds. 2002. *The Manual of Museum Exhibitions*. Walnut Creek, CA: AltaMira Press, 119.

4. Bachmann, Konstanze. 2012. *Conservations Concerns: A Guide for Collectors and Curators*. Washington, DC: Smithsonian Books, 22.

5. Bachmann, Konstanze. 2012. *Conservations Concerns: A Guide for Collectors and Curators*. Washington, DC: Smithsonian Books, 29.

6. Bachmann, Konstanze. 2012. *Conservations Concerns: A Guide for Collectors and Curators*. Washington, DC: Smithsonian Books, 17.

7. Matassa, Freda. 2011. *Museum Collections Management*. London: Facet Publishing, 106.

8. Northeast Document Conservation Center. 1999. "2.5 Protecting Paper and Book Collections during Exhibition." Accessed September 1, 2020. https://www.nedcc.org/free-resources/preservation-leaflets/2.-the-environment/2.5-protecting-paper-and-book-collections-during-exhibition.

9. Matassa, Freda. 2011. *Museum Collections Management*. London: Facet Publishing, 206.

10. Gibbons, Patti. 2015. "Disaster Management and Exhibition Loans: Contingency Planning for Items on Display." In *Handbook of Research on Disaster Management and Contingency Planning in Modern Libraries*, edited by E. Decker and J. Townes. Hershey, PA: IGI-Global, 157–60.

11. Lord, Barry, and Gail Dexter Lord, eds. 2002. *The Manual of Museum Exhibitions*. Walnut Creek, CA: AltaMira Press, 138.

12. Lord, Barry, and Gail Dexter Lord, eds. 2002. *The Manual of Museum Exhibitions*. Walnut Creek, CA: AltaMira Press, 138–39.

13. Lord, Barry, and Gail Dexter Lord, eds. 2002. *The Manual of Museum Exhibitions*. Walnut Creek, CA: AltaMira Press, 139.

14. Smithsonian Institution. 1996. *Smithsonian Guidelines for Accessible Exhibition Design.* Washington, DC: Smithsonian Accessibility Program. Accessed September 1, 2020. https://www .sifacilities.si.edu/sites/default/files/Files/Accessibility/accessible-exhibition-design1.pdf.

15. Hansen, Beth. 2017. *Great Exhibits! An Exhibit Planning and Construction Handbook for Small Museums.* Lanham, MD: AltaMira Press, 71–72.

⊚ References

Bachmann, Konstanze. 2012. *Conservations Concerns: A Guide for Collectors and Curators.* Washington, DC: Smithsonian Books.

Gibbons, Patti. 2015. "Disaster Management and Exhibition Loans: Contingency Planning for Items on Display." In *Handbook of Research on Disaster Management and Contingency Planning in Modern Libraries*, edited by E. Decker and J. Townes. Hershey, PA: IGI-Global.

Hansen, Beth. 2017. *Great Exhibits! An Exhibit Planning and Construction Handbook for Small Museums.* Lanham, MD: AltaMira Press.

Lord, Barry, and Gail Dexter Lord, eds. 2002. *The Manual of Museum Exhibitions.* Walnut Creek, CA: AltaMira Press.

Matassa, Freda. 2011. *Museum Collections Management.* London: Facet Publishing.

Northeast Document Conservation Center. 1999. "2.5 Protecting Paper and Book Collections during Exhibition." Accessed September 1, 2020. https://www.nedcc.org/free-resources/ preservation-leaflets/2.-the-environment/2.5-protecting-paper-and-book-collections-during -exhibition.

Northeast Document Conservation Center. 2012. "2.4 Protection from Light Damage." Accessed September 1, 2020. https://www.nedcc.org/free-resources/preservation-leaflets/2.-the -environment/2.4-protection-from-light-damage.

Smithsonian Institution. 1996. *Smithsonian Guidelines for Accessible Exhibition Design.* Washington, DC: Smithsonian Accessibility Program. Accessed September 1, 2020. https://www .sifacilities.si.edu/sites/default/files/Files/Accessibility/accessible-exhibition-design1.pdf.

Resources Mentioned in This Chapter

AIC (American Institute for Conservation) Find a Conservator: https://www.culturalheritage .org/membership/find-a-conservator

Archival supply vendors:

- Conservation Resources International, LLC: http://www.conservationresources.com/
- Gaylord Archival: https://www.gaylord.com/
- Talas Supplies: https://www.talasonline.com/

PMA, positionable mounting adhesive, produced by 3M and available through art supply retailers

⊚ Further Reading

Bogel, Elizabeth. 2013. *Museum Exhibition Planning and Design.* Lanham, MD: AltaMira Press.

Brown, Mary E. 2006. *Exhibits in Libraries: A Practical Guide.* Jefferson, NC: McFarland.

Hughes, Philip. 2015. *Exhibition Design: An Introduction.* London: Laurence King Publishing.

Lacher-Feldman, Jessica L. 2017. *Exhibits in Archives and Special Collections Libraries.* [S.l.]: Society of American Archivists.

Layne, Stevan P. 2014. *Safeguarding Cultural Properties: Security for Museums, Libraries, Parks, and Zoos.* Waltham, MA: Butterworth-Heinemann.

Matassa, Freda. 2014. *Organizing Exhibitions: A Handbook for Museums, Libraries, and Archives.* London: Facet.

McKenna-Cress, Polly, and Janet A. Kamien. 2013. *Creating Exhibitions: Collaboration in the Planning, Development, and Design of Innovative Experiences.* Hoboken, NJ: John Wiley & Sons.

Powell, Brent A. 2016. *Collection Care: An Illustrated Handbook for the Care and Handling of Cultural Objects.* Lanham, MD: Rowman & Littlefield.

Stringer, Katie. 2014. *Programming for People with Special Needs: A Guide for Museums and Historic Sites.* Lanham, MD: Rowman & Littlefield.

Wilkie, Everett C. 2011. *Guide to Security Considerations & Practices for Rare Book, Manuscript, and Special Collections Libraries.* Chicago: Association of Research Libraries.

CHAPTER 6

Bring It In!

Loans, Traveling Shows, and Pop-Up Exhibits

NO MATTER HOW COMPLETE your collection holdings are, exhibitions may prompt you to borrow materials from other libraries or individuals to help tell your story. The perfect item might be at another library, or an individual collector may have a finer example of an important work, or your item is needed for teaching and instruction during the exhibition period. Sometimes, too, exhibits can excite partners and potential donors, and borrowing materials may be the first step in forging a future philanthropic relationship. Borrowing materials can be a way to enrich your exhibit and perhaps strengthen ties with your community.

Your library can also book traveling exhibitions. Being a venue allows you to host exhibits produced by larger organizations that travel in a circuit. Traveling shows may help you tell stories that are interesting to your audience but lay outside of your collection scope or staff expertise. Most libraries do not have the capacity to produce slick exhibits with enticing hands-on interactives and immersive environments. Renting traveling exhibits can bring museum-quality environments to your library and dazzle your audience.

Exhibits, too, can be much smaller in scope and temporary pop-up exhibits might appeal to your programming aims. Pop-up exhibits and displays are temporary in nature, require less planning, can be produced guerrilla-style, and often are tied to promotion and outreach for other things. Perhaps you have a new idea to test-drive; a small pop-up exhibit may help. If you have a large theme that you would like to cover in a series of smaller exhibits rather than a larger show, you can stagger a rotation of small pop-ups. Sometimes people or groups may approach you with ideas for time-sensitive displays that are hard to fit into your existing schedule or are too small to fill your venue, and pop-up exhibits can help you accommodate these opportunities.

Building Partnerships

Loans can help foster relationships between your library and other libraries, archives, and museums.[1] Through cross-programming, you may expand your constituency base and widen partnerships. Loans, especially local and regional loans, can help establish a reciprocal network with loans and promote an overall awareness of services.

Traveling exhibit costs can be steep, but partnering with others on exhibitions can stretch resources. Pairing with granting agencies in your community, state government, or national agencies can bring quality programming to your library patrons and help establish avenues of support for future projects.[2]

Exhibit loans made with individuals can help you get to know bibliophiles and collectors in your region or collecting area, and allow them to learn about your institution, its scope, and daily practices. Many lenders become donors, especially when they respect the mission of your organization, the professionalism of your staff, and feel personally connected to successful outreach projects, such as exhibits.

Similarly, pop-up exhibits give you an opportunity to meet and work with people or groups in your community who are grateful to have impromptu space to express their ideas and art, and to access your audience. By listening to pop-up creators and getting feedback from their work, you gain a deeper understanding of your audience and perhaps grow it with new streams of visitors coming to the library for the pop-up show. Overall, loans of all sorts are excellent ways to partner with like-minded groups and expand offerings for your visitors (see figures 6.1 and 6.2).

Loan Policies and Contracts

Loan Policies

Established exhibition loan policies are immensely useful and are prudent resources that help you evaluate legal agreements and guide you through contract terms. For the scope of this chapter, the discussion is limited to *incoming* loan policies and agreements that cover materials your library is borrowing. (*It is equally important to develop policies and procedures covering* outgoing *loans of materials leaving your library*.)

Your incoming loan policy is an internal document that details the requirements your library establishes for arranging, approving, and handling materials it borrows for exhibitions. The policy should guide staff through the negotiation process and help them evaluate whether an agreement fits within the institution's mission and is free of legal risks.

Figure 6.1. Kite exhibit by artist Scott Hampton; on display at Sandy Library, Sandy, Utah. *Scott Hampton.*

INCOMING LOAN POLICY TOPICS

- Mission of exhibit program
- Scope of what you will borrow
- Partnerships, who you will borrow from
- Long-term loan policy
- Shipping and packing methods
- Staff authorized to sign contracts and handle materials
- Storage and handling protocols
- Procedures to decline or request additional terms

Loan Agreement Form

Most lenders will present you with their loan forms or contracts. As the borrower, you should use their documents exclusively and strictly defer to all terms. In some cases, you may need to provide a borrower with loan forms. For instance, most individuals do not have personal contracts and smaller organizations may not have loan forms. For those

Figure 6.2. Kite exhibit by artist Scott Hampton; on display at Sandy Library, Sandy, Utah. *Scott Hampton.*

occasions, it is helpful to develop incoming loan forms. With all legal documents, it is advisable to have your organization's legal counsel review the document to ensure it protects your library sufficiently.

Incoming loan agreements should explicitly state the terms of the loan; address physical care needs for the borrowed materials; and detail coverage of loan-related costs, insurance requirements, and notes on photography or image needs relating to the exhibition.

INFORMATION TO INCLUDE ON
AN INCOMING LOAN AGREEMENT FORM

- Header with library's contact information, logo, and form's title

  - Lender's contact information
  - Full institution name
  - Address

- Contact person's name and title

  - Telephone number
  - E-mail address

- Purpose of loan

  - Exhibit title
  - Dates of loan
  - Venue(s)

- Insurance information

  - Library to provide insurance coverage, lender to insure and provide certificate prior to shipping, or lender waives insurance coverage
  - Total value to insure loan
  - Value of individual pieces

- Return shipping information

  - Ship to address
  - Ship to the attention of contact person
  - Preferred shipping date
  - Transit carrier requirements
  - Shipping stipulations, instructions, and notes

- Description of objects and condition notes

  - Call number or inventory number
  - Author/artist
  - Title of work
  - Date
  - Dimensions
  - Weight
  - Auxiliary dimensions (framing notes)
  - General condition
  - Installation and exhibition instructions

- Credit line and copyright

  - Wording for labels
  - Photography stipulations and copyright terms

- Additional loan conditions and terms

Traveling Exhibit and Pop-Up Contracts

Large cultural heritage organizations such as the Smithsonian Institution, the New York Public Library, and the American Library Association, along with individual museums and some libraries, develop and travel complete shows as part of their outreach mission. Traveling exhibits are fee based, and provide a "turnkey" exhibition experience.

Traveling exhibitions can be small-scale productions or complex installations that require thousands of square feet of space.[3] Components can be oversized, contain living animals, or require power or data inputs. As you research a traveling exhibition, carefully examine the details so you know the sizes and types of items displayed, along with all shipping, installation, and maintenance needs.

- Do you have sufficient space to install and display the installation at your library?
- Are components freestanding, or do they need to be anchored to walls or floors?
- Do you have the staff and equipment needed to install and maintain the exhibit?
- What are the dimensions of the shipping containers, and will these fit through your library's doors and hallways?

When borrowing entire exhibits from a traveling exhibition program, the exhibit owners or group managing its travel will work with you to book the show. Bookings generally begin with an application where you provide details about your organization, your audience, and your physical facility.[4] When rare book or sensitive materials travel, owners generally have additional environmental-, conservation-, and security-related requirements. You likely will need to provide a detailed facility report (see Loan Registration below).

If your application is approved, booking agents will forward a contract to you. Traveling exhibition contracts cover terms such as shipping/receiving, insurance, assembly, maintenance, promotion, and terms of liability. Be sure to read the contract carefully to assure that your organization can meet requirements. As needed, negotiate terms with the booking agent to your mutual satisfaction.

When completing your contract, booking agents will create a payment schedule. Typically a deposit of about 25 percent is required to secure your booking, and final payments and a certificate of insurance are due before materials ship.[5]

External pop-up exhibit creators may contact the library for temporary exhibition space. Arrangements may be informal, and it would be appropriate to use your library's incoming loan agreement. If the creator has a contract for the pop-up exhibit, review all terms and conditions carefully. Pop-up exhibits typically do not have fee-based rental agreements. Curators of these displays tend to seek exposure and collaborate without charge.

⌾ Loan Registration

Museums employ full-time registration staff to oversee all aspects of the loan process. Most libraries do not have registrars, and must build staff expertise to oversee loans.

Loan registration involves everything from negotiating loans, finalizing loan agreements and contracts, itemizing terms, coordinating insurance, enumerating packing/shipping requirements, documenting item conditions, and specifying lender credit lines. The following are tips for staff overseeing loans.

Negotiation and Formal Requesting Procedures

Many libraries post their exhibit loan policies on their public websites. Researching an organization's lending policies and application process will assist negotiations and let you know upfront whether a loan may be possible. Rare book libraries have more stringent requirements. After reviewing the lending policies, contact the potential lender by following their procedures and providing as full information as possible. Typically, you will need to begin the negotiation months to even a year or more in advance. Loans from an individual or smaller organizations may be markedly less formal. Potential lenders may need the following information in order to evaluate a loan request:

- Organization and contact information
- Exhibition title, overview of the exhibit, and display dates
- Curatorial staff preparing the exhibit and their credentials
- Detailed information about requested item(s), such as call number, title, and page opening for printed materials, and collection, box, and folder information for archival items
- Indications for any published catalog or website projects using images of materials
- Statement of willingness to cover loan-related expenses and uphold terms set forth by the lender

Facility Report

To evaluate a borrower's capacity to adequately care for materials, lenders need information about your library's programs, staffing, environmental controls, and security operations. This information is detailed in a facility report. The American Alliance of Museums' General Facility Report is widely used by cultural heritage organizations.

Registration Details

Registrars oversee loan details that keep materials safe and account for items throughout the entire duration of a loan. Museum registrars maintain a logbook for loans. They issue each loan a unique identification number for tracking purposes. Loan numbers often begin with the code IL (incoming loan), followed by the four-digit year, then listing a sequential number. The first incoming loan of 2021 would be numbered IL2021.1, the second would be IL2021.2, and so on.

For each loan, registrars maintain paper and electronic folders, the contents of each include the following:

- Correspondence
- Loan agreements and contracts
- Insurance certificates

- Itemized list of borrowed items including item dimensions, conditions, and photographs
- Condition reports
- Packing information
- Shipping manifests
- Copies of printed exhibit matter such as brochures or PR clippings

This level of formality may not be necessary to oversee loans at your library, but being aware of the scope of a more robust loan registration operation will inform your decision-making and help you structure your record keeping.

When coordinating a loan, registrars work with lenders to identify special handling and display criteria. Lenders may specify environmental conditions, and they may prescribe how to mount an item. Registrars ensure these mandates are upheld to the satisfaction of the lender.

Similarly, during the loan coordination period, registrars work with lenders to specify packing and shipping arrangements. Some circulating library materials may travel via Inter-Library Loan, but archival and special collections materials should only be transported by those trained in packing and shipping fine art materials. Specialty art-handling companies can build rugged archival containers and crates, and have a secure, established network of shipping methods to move materials safely from door to door.

Registrars work with the library's insurance company to establish what is known as wall-to-wall or nail-to-nail insurance policies that cover borrowed materials throughout the complete loan cycle.[6] Lenders provide valuations and the insurance company can provide certificates of insurance to the owners. Registrars act as a liaison for information and ensure certificates reach the lender in advance of the shipping date. Not all materials need additional fine art insurance. Some libraries' operating insurance policies cover borrowed materials, but this may be limited to circulating collection materials.[7]

To honor loan partners, it is important to ask lenders how they would like to be acknowledged in the exhibit's labels and printed matter. Registrars record this information in the loan agreement forms and contracts. Some individuals may wish to remain anonymous, some lenders would like to honor their entire family, and others may have preferences for nicknames or using honorifics. Traveling exhibits may require the use of logos and marketing icons in exhibition signage and print materials.

Delivery, Installation, Deinstallation, and Maintenance

Couriers

Some lenders will require a courier to accompany items throughout the transportation process and installation. Typically, this is an exhibition or conservation staff person experienced with object handling. Be sure to clearly define the courier's role and duties during the negotiation phase. Some lenders want their courier to place items inside cases, others ask that they oversee the installation process. Typically, the borrower is responsible for covering the courier's travel fees, lodging, and per diem, and generally, couriers are required only for high-value or complicated loans.

With complex traveling shows, often, exhibit preparator staff will accompany the delivery to oversee the unpacking, setup, and repacking. Similarly, with some pop-up exhibits, the exhibit curator, creator, or organizer may be invested in the setup and will collaborate or directly handle the loan delivery, unpacking, setup, and repacking themselves. Below are notes, mostly addressing the needs of rare or high-value items, though the advice can be applied to all types of loan materials.

Delivery

During the loan negotiation stage, the lender will stipulate the mode of delivery. Local loans might be couriered by the owner or your institution's staff directly to the library at an agreed upon day and time. Other loans, especially those further away, generally need transportation arrangements. Rare book and unique materials should not be sent by post or through regular commercial shippers, and most fine art insurance companies prohibit using these carriers. Dedicated fine art shippers are trained and equipped to safely pack and transport valuable library and other cultural heritage materials and have networks in place to broker international shipments if needed. With all loans, it is helpful to contact lenders upon arrival to confirm receipt of shipment.

Traveling exhibit companies or staff overseeing traveling exhibits will work with you in advance on shipping and delivery logistics. Often, traveling exhibits come to you from a previous venue, and staff from that location will contact you to make arrangements. Similarly, you will arrange shipment to the next venue after your show, and it is important to confirm those arrangements as soon as possible.[8]

Unpacking

Museums follow a professional best practice to let materials acclimate and remain fully packed for twenty-four hours after arrival to allow materials to slowly adjust to the new environment. If fragile materials were rushed through varying temperature and humidity ranges, there is a potential for them to crack or break. This best practice helps protect artifacts, particularly wooden, ivory, or other sensitive materials such as rare books with leather and vellum bindings. It is also important to lock materials safely into a room or secure space during the waiting period, and to remember to build in an extra day for material acclimation.

Upon arrival, inspect the package and crate exteriors for signs of damage. Photo-document the condition of shipping containers and write notes of any signs of trouble. With signs of explicit damage, contact the lender immediately for instructions on how to proceed.

In most cases, containers arrive in wonderful condition and are ready to unpack after the acclimation period. Work in a secure staff space, optimally one limited to the exhibition team working on the project. Carefully open and document the contents. Be sure to note how materials are packed, in what order, and in what position. A combination of snapshots and detailed written notes will record how items were packed and be of great help to you when you repack materials at the end of the loan.

As you work, carefully place items aside and check items off your master item list. Once you confirm that all materials have arrived and are unpacked, you can store containers in a secure, low-traffic area. If items are crated, be sure to fasten lids to prevent wooden parts from warping.

With traveling exhibits, it is important to document how materials arrive and the manner they are packed. The notes establish condition upon receipt, and will aid in the repacking phase after the exhibit.

Condition Reporting

You need to document each item's physical condition as received. Some lenders will send you condition reports they prepared immediately before the item was packed for the loan (see figure 6.3). With those notes in hand, examine each piece and compare what you see to the lender's observations. If the lender did not send condition reports, you can document "as delivered" conditions using your own item condition report form, making sure to capture the following:

- Loan number
- Name of lender
- Exhibition name
- Name of item
- Identifying number such as a call number
- Measurements
- Description of parts
- Detailed notes and description of any flaws or damage
- Sketches of flaws detailing placement
- Your name
- Date of the report

Use a camera to photo-document materials and sketch items and the placement of flaws. If you are using the lender's condition reports, note any additional observations on the form, followed by your initials and date.

Similarly, with traveling exhibitions, it is important to inspect all components for damage and to document and communicate problems to the organizer.

Installation

Loans may arrive from days to weeks in advance, depending on the terms brokered. The additional time may be needed to have the item onsite in order to create mounts, though some lenders send custom mounts as part of the loan.

With thorough planning, you will create an installation schedule, including the details of loaned materials. It is helpful to document the installation with photographs. You can share photos with the lender, though this generally is not required.

Traveling and pop-up exhibits can present complex installations. Lenders or their representatives may be needed onsite to oversee or execute the installation.

Deinstallation

Weeks prior to the installation you will coordinate with the lender to finalize and confirm return shipping arrangements. Similarly, with traveling exhibits or pop-ups, you work in advance to confirm deinstallation details, and the lender's staff may return to dismantle and repack exhibits.

After a successful exhibition, you carefully dismount your exhibit, make condition reports for items and note any physical changes, and repack materials exactly as received at the start of the loan. With condition reporting, it is also prudent to photograph items during the deinstallation work, and to photograph the sealed packing containers. Send

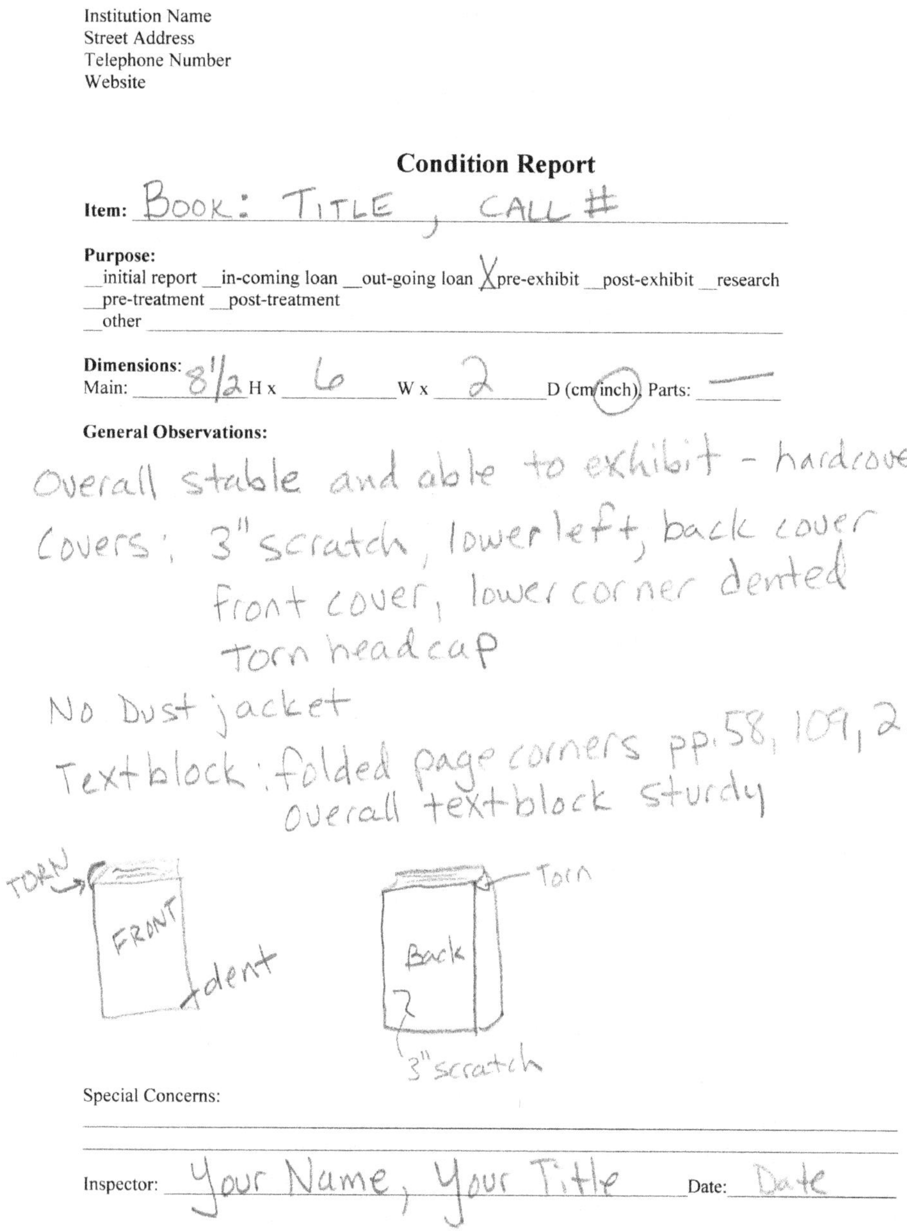

Institution Name
Street Address
Telephone Number
Website

Condition Report

Item: Book: Title , Call #

Purpose:
__initial report __in-coming loan __out-going loan X pre-exhibit __post-exhibit __research
__pre-treatment __post-treatment
__other _____

Dimensions:
Main: 8 1/2 H x 6 W x 2 D (cm/inch) Parts: —

General Observations:

Overall stable and able to exhibit - hardcover book
Covers: 3" scratch, lower left, back cover
 front cover, lower corner dented
 torn headcap
No Dust jacket
Textblock: folded page corners pp. 58, 109, 217
 overall textblock sturdy

TORN → FRONT dent   Torn
                    Back
                    3" scratch

Special Concerns: _____

Inspector: Your Name, Your Title   **Date:** Date

Figure 6.3. Sample condition report with notes and sketches detailing imperfections and their locations. *Patti Gibbons.*

lenders their original condition reports with your incoming and outgoing notes, making sure to retain a copy for your records. If you are using your own condition reporting forms, keep the original and send lenders a copy. In the event that any damage is discovered, document the change thoroughly and contact the lender immediately to discuss next steps.

Maintenance

It is essential with all borrowed materials to protect and uphold original conditions. Do not clean or conserve materials. If you observe material flaws or damage, notify the lender immediately and await next steps. It is prudent to include contingency plans for loan material in your institutional disaster planning. Know how to react with loan materials.

These discussions can be part of the conversation you have with lenders during the loan negotiation phases.

Traveling exhibits typically cover maintenance details in the contract. Contracts also include information about repairs and troubleshooting interactive components. The organization traveling the exhibit will address service issues. Refer problems to your contact with the traveling exhibit program.

Definitions

- Facility report—a comprehensive questionnaire that details a cultural heritage institution's facilities, security protocols, programs, and staff credentials as relating to evaluating capacity to borrow materials
- Loan registration—the comprehensive procedures taken to plan, coordinate, and oversee a formal exhibition loan, which includes brokering loans, completing loan agreements/contracts, specifying terms, and maintaining records. In museums, this work is completed by a registrar
- Pop-up exhibit—short-term exhibition or display, generally less formal than traditional exhibitions and might be curated by community stakeholders or self-trained curators; often ephemeral in nature and planned quickly in response to current events

Key Points

- Overall, loans of all sorts are excellent ways to partner with like-minded groups and people to expand offerings for your visitors
- The incoming loan policy is an internal document that details the requirements your library establishes for arranging, approving, and handling materials it borrows for exhibitions
- Loan registration involves negotiating loans, finalizing agreements and contracts, itemizing terms, coordinating insurance, specifying packing/shipping details, receiving materials, documenting conditions, and specifying item and lender credit lines
- Follow all terms lenders specify for loan packing, shipping, unpacking, installation, maintenance, and deinstallation

Notes

1. Hildebrandt, Beth, Stacey Knight-Davis, J. J. Pionke, and Andrew Cougill. 2019. "Designs of Duty: Using Exhibits to Build Partnerships." *College & Undergraduate Libraries.* 26 (1): 52–65.

2. Kobayashi, Evelyn, and MaryJoy Rojo. 2018. "A Small Library's Playbook for Hosting NLM Traveling Exhibits." *Journal of Hospital Librarianship.* 18 (1): 38–46.

3. Brown, Mary E., and Rebecca Power. 2006. *Exhibits in Libraries: A Practical Guide.* Jefferson, NC: McFarland, 156.

4. Brown, Mary E., and Rebecca Power. 2006. *Exhibits in Libraries: A Practical Guide.* Jefferson, NC: McFarland, 160–62.

5. Brown, Mary E., and Rebecca Power. 2006. *Exhibits in Libraries: A Practical Guide.* Jefferson, NC: McFarland, 162–63.

6. Gibbons, Patti. 2015. "Disaster Management and Exhibition Loans: Contingency Planning for Items on Display." In *Handbook of Research on Disaster Management and Contingency Planning in Modern Libraries*, edited by E. Decker and J. Townes. Hershey, PA: IGI-Global, 150–51.

7. Gibbons, Patti. 2015. "Disaster Management and Exhibition Loans: Contingency Planning for Items on Display." In *Handbook of Research on Disaster Management and Contingency Planning in Modern Libraries*, edited by E. Decker and J. Townes. Hershey, PA: IGI-Global, 150.

8. Brown, Mary E., and Rebecca Power. 2006. *Exhibits in Libraries: A Practical Guide.* Jefferson, NC: McFarland, 164.

References

Brown, Mary E., and Rebecca Power. 2006. *Exhibits in Libraries: A Practical Guide.* Jefferson, NC: McFarland.

Gibbons, Patti. 2015. "Disaster Management and Exhibition Loans: Contingency Planning for Items on Display." In *Handbook of Research on Disaster Management and Contingency Planning in Modern Libraries*, edited by E. Decker and J. Townes. Hershey, PA: IGI-Global.

Hildebrandt, Beth, Stacey Knight-Davis, J. J. Pionke, and Andrew Cougill. 2019. "Designs of Duty: Using Exhibits to Build Partnerships." *College & Undergraduate Libraries.* 26 (1): 52–65.

Kobayashi, Evelyn, and MaryJoy Rojo. 2018. "A Small Library's Playbook for Hosting NLM Traveling Exhibits." *Journal of Hospital Librarianship.* 18 (1): 38–46.

Resources Mentioned in This Chapter

ALA (American Library Association) traveling exhibits: http://www.ala.org/tools/programming/exhibitions

AAM (American Alliance of Museums) General Facility Report: https://ww2.aam-us.org/Product Catalog/Product?ID=891

New York Public Library traveling exhibits: https://www.nypl.org/about/locations/schomburg/traveling-exhibitions

SITES (Smithsonian Institution Traveling Exhibition Service): https://www.sites.si.edu/s/

Further Reading

Buck, Rebecca A. 2011. *MRM5: Museum Registration Methods.* Washington, DC: AAM Press.

Buck, Rebecca A., and Jean Allman Gilmore. 2003. *On the Road Again: Developing and Managing Traveling Exhibitions.* Washington, DC: AAM Press.

Malaro, Marie C., and Ildiko Pogany DeAngelis. 2012. *A Legal Primer on Managing Museum Collections.* Washington, DC: Smithsonian Books.

Powell, Susan, and Samantha Teplitzky. 2016. "Pop-Up Exhibits as an Outreach Tool: Connecting Academic and Public Audiences with Library Resources." UC Berkeley: Library. Accessed September 1, 2020. https://escholarship.org/uc/item/8bh1p8nn.

Reibel, Daniel B. 2018. *Registration Methods for the Small Museum.* Lanham, MD: Rowman & Littlefield.

Settocucato, Elizabeth, Ruth Ann Jones, and Cindy Krolikowski. 2017. "Seminar D: Every Space Is Special: The Art and Science of Pop-Up Special Collections Exhibits." RBMS (Rare Book Manuscript Section of the American Library Association), Iowa City, IA, June 20–23.

Simmons, John E. 2020. *Museum Registration Methods.* Washington, DC: American Alliance of Museums.

CHAPTER 7

Click It!

Digital Exhibits

IN THIS CHAPTER

▷ Opportunities and differences

▷ Digital exhibit development

▷ Structure, design, and accessibility

▷ Copyright

▷ Open source tools

VIRTUAL EXHIBITS ARE CONSUMED AT HOME and on the go, from computers, tablets, and phones rather than at the library, but still interpret and highlight your collection materials. In many aspects, these web exhibits are similar in aim and experience to physical exhibitions, but their dissimilarities present unique opportunities that help you reach audiences differently. Digital exhibit content is discoverable online and provides another avenue to promote collection holdings and encourage visitors to come to the library.

Opportunities and Differences

You can develop digital exhibitions in conjunction with physical shows, or create sites that tackle subjects independent of a gallery experience. When designing web exhibits to accompany shows, remember that web exhibits are not a one-to-one representation. They capture the essence of an exhibit but are their own experience. Also, you can produce web exhibits to discuss topics outside the subjects you explore in physical exhibits and displays.

Virtual exhibits can help you provide a ready reference resource for recurring questions on hot topics, or help you showcase important holdings. As physical pop-up exhibits, digital sites can be assembled relatively quickly and respond to issues in a more timely manner than physical exhibitions.

Audience

Through virtual exhibitions, you can connect with audiences beyond your building and outside the run of an exhibition timeframe. Remote visits can occur around the clock, across the globe, and into perpetuity, whereas visits to physical exhibits are limited to business hours during the run of a show. You can continually refer people to your web exhibitions. Removing barriers of time and space allows for wide, open access to your content.

Size

When you design web exhibits, you control the scale. Web exhibits can be attractive and useful as limited pages or as larger, more robust sites. Dealing in virtual space, you do not face physical limits to fit into confined areas or expand wall-to-wall to fill an entire room.

Physical Considerations

Web exhibits can help you get around preservation issues that prevent you from displaying items or presenting them over lengthy periods of time. Issues of lighting, environmental exposure, and security are avoided. Nicely, many older collection gems in rare book libraries that face stringent display guidelines predate copyright restrictions and are wonderful inclusions in digital exhibitions.

Because you do not display original physical items in a web exhibit, you have the benefit of controlling the size of digital images. You are able to enlarge small items to provide prominence or focus on details that could be overlooked in person.

Digital Exhibit Development

Just as with physical exhibits, you need to develop and research virtual web exhibits thoroughly. During your planning stages, start with an idea or theme and identify a particular angle to explore. Have something new to say or cover ground that provides answers or insights to often-inquired-about information relating to your holdings. Just as with physical exhibits, when planning web exhibitions, take time to map out broad learning objectives and determine the key messages you want visitors to take away from their virtual visit. Having a solid handle on the aims and objectives of the site will help you select images and text, and make design and layout choices that make an effective and engaging site.

You may find benefit in partnering with others to create web exhibitions. Academic librarians might collaborate with instructors to integrate virtual exhibition development into course projects. Student-curated shows present new information, while also providing students with a firsthand experience researching, evaluating, and summarizing collection materials.

Audience and Analytics

Unlike physical exhibits where visitors come to your facilities, web visitors can be located anywhere. Web guests can be of any demographic and may be unfamiliar with your library's programs, services, or community. Visitors may speak other languages and could be using a translating app to access information. Compared to exhibit visitors you meet on-site, you will know less about your virtual visitors.

Web analytics, such as Google Analytics, measure and quantify web data that can help you understand web traffic and use patterns (see figure 7.1). Reviewing analytics will help you learn more about your web audience and their visitation patterns. Through analytics, you can study the average length of time on pages, geographic location of visitors, and bounce rate, among other statistics.[1] Study what works and see what is popular. You can use analytics to track trends over time, and you can adjust your exhibitions using the information and insights gleaned through website analytics.

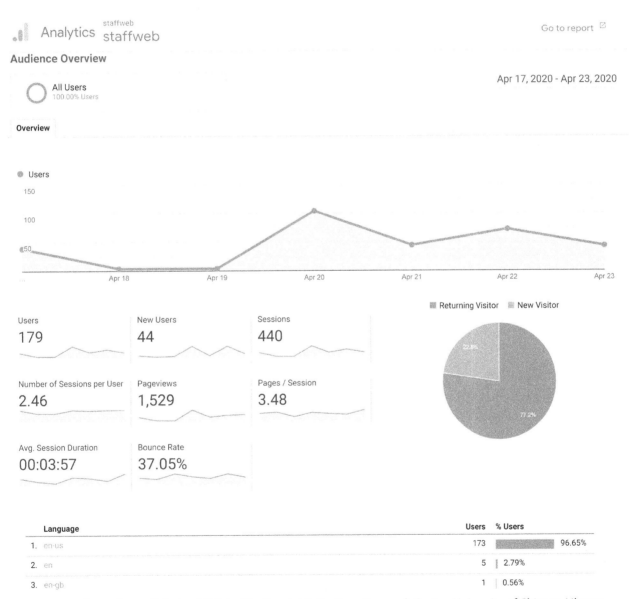

Figure 7.1. Data about digital exhibit traffic. *Special Collections Research Center, University of Chicago Library.*

Content Length

If you overwhelm or bore virtual visitors with dense text, they will likely click away. While the golden rule of brevity still holds true, with digital exhibits, word counts are not as strict or prescribed as best practice guidelines for labels in physical exhibits. In fact, web exhibits can be a great place to park a subject's richer and more detailed information that did not make it into a physical exhibit because of space or perhaps because the content was too granular to appeal to a general gallery visitor. For instance, in your web exhibitions, you can include bibliographies for further reading and links to groups, organizations, or resources related to a particular topic.

In-House Policies and Procedures

Your library may find it helpful to establish formal policies and procedures to guide your virtual exhibition program. The policy could include the following:

- Mission and aims of the program
- Details on how your organization vets proposals for web exhibitions and evaluates subject matter
- An enumeration of staff responsibilities for design, maintenance, migration to new platforms, and web archiving
- Style guide specifics for design conventions
- ADA compliance review steps

Style Guide

Keeping a consistent look throughout your web exhibitions and having them feel related to your larger website promotes your organization's branding aims. Regularity helps visitors navigate and recognize that they are in your library's site. Taking time to decide on visual standards promotes uniformity, and you can document design choices and preferences in a web exhibit style guide. Guides can speak to structural components such as placement of navigation menus, as well as font usage, logo placement, and in-house conventions for crediting images, people, or materials.

Cascading Style Sheets

Web designers rely on CSS, cascading style sheets, to standardize the visual presentation of web pages. CSS is the language that adapts the presentation of color, fonts, layout, and sizing to different device types—such as wide screens, small screens, and printers—and keeps visual presentation uniform across pages and devices. CSS is used in conjunction with XML markup language to keep headers, subheaders, and section structures consistent in terms of size, color, and font. Beyond visual presentation clarity, CSS maintains hierarchies and directly aids in screen reading for visually assisted navigation.[2]

Structure, Design, and Accessibility

Virtual exhibits can be built from the ground up, created from web exhibition-specific software (*see Open Source Tools*), or be a hybrid where you modified open source structures to meet your needs. As an organization, you will decide if you have the in-house expertise needed to build web exhibits or if using a product is more sensible. If you are designing a site, tour the web and see what other libraries and museums have created. Pay attention to layouts, colors, image use, tone, length, and technical features. Be influenced. If it appeals to you, that is a nice place to start your design work.

Basic Site Features

Structuring pages organizes information and aids intuitive navigation. Web exhibition structures commonly include the following:

- Page menu, or list of contents
- Home page
- Content pages
- Acknowledgments and credits page
- About this exhibit page
- Graphic logos or visual page header/footer motifs that appear consistently across the digital exhibit's child pages
- Links to your library's home page and catalog
- Contact information and branding logos

Across your site, give consideration to how you would like people to navigate from page to page. Do you want people to move horizontally or vertically through pages? When designing versions for mobile devices, you will create fluid designs that reshape the layout depending on the orientation and resolution the user selects for their screen.[3] With responsive design, you need to plan for a range of sizes and decide where you want features, such as the navigation bar and content, to fall on screen sizes of small through enlarged dimensions.

When designing pages, you map the importance of titles, section dividers, and context areas using a visual hierarchy structure (see figure 7.2). It is important to employ CSS settings to maintain consistency. Heading sections use large fonts, and perhaps bolded or differently colored typeface, to distinguish them from other content. Subsections use slightly smaller and possibly italics or colored text. Variations in size, weight, style, and color help organize sections visually and guide visitors through content. During design phases, you will also select text colors and fonts. Choose high contrasting color combinations so text is easy to read against colored backgrounds.

During the design phase, you will also size and position graphics and images. Images break up text and make pages appealing. Dense, text-dominant pages are difficult to read. Be sure to leave enough "white space" free of content to provide visitors with a visual break.

Interactive features engage users and encourage longer site visits. Zooming capabilities allow visitors to home in on details and explore graphics. Image carousels and slideshows present visual content that is eye-catching and can quickly hook visitors. Including image collections that visitors roam through keeps top-level pages tidy and allows you to nest a group of images rather than display them as a series, which could grow to unmanageable lengths if there are numerous images.

Beyond graphic imagery, you can enhance user experience and provide more information through media. Including audio and film clips conveys a different range of information and provides a variety of learning experiences.

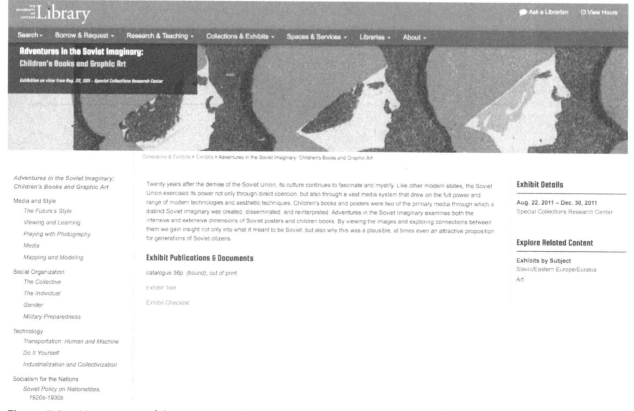

Figure 7.2. Home page of the University of Chicago Library's *Adventures in the Soviet Imaginary* digital exhibition. Notice the navigation menu along the left, detailing additional pages. *Special Collections Research Center, University of Chicago Library.*

Creating Accessible Content through Design

Being aware of barriers to use allows you to create digital exhibitions free of obstacles that hamper visitors' experiences.[4] Web Content Accessibility Guidelines (WCAG) provide standards for web accessibility that can guide your work.[5] The WCAG are organized into four principles, stating that for all users on a range of devices, that web content must be:

- Perceivable
- Operable
- Understandable
- Robust[6]

Perceivable

Aptly labeling images and graphic elements provides context when visitors access a web exhibition with a screen reader. Known as *alt text*, these descriptive captions provide information about the visual elements displayed on a screen. With alt text, aim to present content and function, not necessarily a description of an image. Avoid empty phrases such as "picture of" or "image of," and describe images succinctly. Search engines harvest alt text, and the richer your information, the better for readers and for overall discoverability.

Audio and video materials are not universally perceivable. Sound elements should include closed captioning and videos should be accompanied by transcriptions in order to convey content in an alternative format. Professional transcription services are fee based, but sites such as YouTube provide free automatic captioning that generally requires additional editing to improve accuracy.

To promote legibility, sites need to have sufficient contrast between text and background colors. Employ color and pattern when emphasizing differences onscreen because not all viewers can distinguish color variants. While color greatly impacts and adds to the virtual exhibition experience, it can present barriers if not used effectively. Online tools such as WebAIM's Contrast Checker and Coblis Color Blindness Simulator help identify problematic color combinations to improve legibility.

Recommendations to make content perceivable to users include the following:

- Providing alt text for non-text material
- Including captions and transcripts for multimedia
- Making materials easier for users to see through high contrast between color and background[7]

Operable

Users need to navigate a site freely, and design features should be intuitive and provide two or more ways to explore content such as through a site map and search feature. Not all visitors use a mouse, and keyboard accessibility is an essential navigation tool. Users should be able to rely on keyboards to access menus and links, and web pages need a visible indicator, such as a cursor, to identify positioning on a keyboard.[8]

If your site includes slideshows or image carousels, it is helpful to include generous autoscroll timing and a pause feature to allow users ample time to view images. Flashing images can be jarring to viewers and may prompt seizures, and they should be avoided.[9]

Recommendations to make content operable to users include the following:

- Support intuitive navigation
- All content should be keyboard navigable
- Set generous intervals for slideshows or timed components
- Do not include strobes or flashing components that prompt seizures[10]

Understandable

Semantic elements of web pages need to communicate structure such as headings, subheadings, and lists. Section elements need to distinguish and present an intuitive and logical reading order. Overall content organization helps visitors navigate through pages and the use of CSS structural markup language will order how screen readers move through text hierarchies.[11]

If listing information, employ numbered lists to indicate rank and bulleted lists if there is no weighted order.[12]

To help insure your text is understandable to most, give thought to the general reading level. Online sites such as Readable evaluate text and gauge reading levels.

Recommendations to make content understandable to users include the following:

- Structure, design, and layout should help users avoid and correct mistakes
- Site operation and content appearance should be predictable
- Text should be understandable and readable[13]

Robust

Content needs to be reliably interpreted by a range of users and assistive technologies.[14] Structures need to be robust and sophisticated in order to maximize compatibility with the current and future technologies users employ to access a site. Continually review web structures to assess the viability of its structure and utility.

Recommendations to ensure robust content is available for users include the following:

- Valid HTML coding used for pages
- ARIA markup used with dynamic components such as slideshows and dropdown menus[15]

Evaluating Accessibility

Utah State University created a web accessibility evaluation tool called WAVE. It is a free instrument you can employ to appraise website accessibility. WAVE flags shortcomings such as contrast errors, inconsistent header hierarchy, missing alternative text, unordered lists, and uncaptioned video files.

ⓖ Copyright

Unlike in a physical exhibit where you display your copy of a book or original materials from your archive, digital presentations are a form of publication and copyright is something to review earnestly. Grappling with copyright considerations is familiar territory for many librarians, and online exhibitions present challenges. You need to assess copyright for images, audio, video, and text passages. You must secure permissions to use protected materials in virtual exhibits.

Lawyer Richard Stim identifies five steps to copyright review:

- Determine if permission is needed
- Identify owner
- Identify rights needed

- Contact owner and negotiate payment
- Get permission in writing[16]

To determine whether permission is needed, Stim states, "You should always start with the presumption that, if the creative work you want to use was first published after 1922, U.S. copyright law protects it."[17] Works published after 1922 fall outside of copyright only if the owner failed to renew copyright protection, or if the work did not meet minimum copyright standards.[18] (*See Public Domain and Fair Use below for more information.*)

To identify a rights owner, as a starting point, look for a copyright statement on the material. Ownership may have changed hands since the date of publication, and note that music, film, artwork, and materials created outside of the United States often are more complex than domestically published printed works and may have multiple rights holders, such as recording companies, music publishers, and artists' estates.[19]

As you seek permissions for web use, you will specify whether you need exclusive or nonexclusive use, and general terms of use, such as length of time and territory or country of use.[20] While you are discussing terms with the rights owner, you will also negotiate fees if applicable. Be sure to get permission and terms of use in writing and document the negotiations.

Public Domain and Fair Use

Public Domain

Creative works that are not protected by copyright laws are in the public domain and can be used freely and do not require permissions.[21] In the United States, copyright has expired for all works created before January 1, 1923, and they can be freely used.[22]

Works published before 1964 entered the public domain if rights were not renewed.[23] Many works were not renewed and can be used without permission. For materials produced between 1922 and 1964, you can research the status of copyright at the U.S. Copyright Office.[24]

Legislation adopted in 1998 has now matured, and works published after January 1, 1923, began entering the public domain in 2019, those created in 1924 expired in 2020, and so on. For works published after 1977, rights will not expire until seventy years after the death of the author or last remaining creator for published works with multiple contributors.[25]

The American Library Association's Public Domain Slider is a useful online instrument designed to help you determine whether a work is protected.

Fair Use

Fair use is a principle founded on the belief that public use of portions of copyright-protected materials is permissible for purposes of criticism and commentary.[26] Copyright holders can challenge fair usage, and courts deliberate cases on an individual basis, weighing the purpose of use, nature of the protected material, amount of material used, and effect of use on a commercial market.[27] The American Library Association's Fair Use Evaluator is a practical tool designed to help you determine copyright status.

Large repositories such as the Creative Commons Database, Flickr Creative Commons, Google Advanced Image Search, and Wikimedia Commons contain images in the public domain. You might mine these sources for images and content to use in your web exhibitions.

As always, with all attributions and use, be sure to cite sources. Beyond identifying images used in your web exhibitions to credit creators, it is helpful to also include your library's identification numbers to help you retrieve specific materials. Reference questions will come in the future when details get fuzzy and staff turn over, and having ready identifiers will be helpful.

⊚ Open Source Tools

Open source platforms and digital asset management systems are great tools to help you build web exhibitions and manage digital collection metadata. Below are a few popular offerings used frequently to create web exhibitions for libraries.[28]

Omeka

Omeka is open source, web-publishing software that offers attractive turnkey templates for web exhibitions and online presentation of digital collections. Omeka offers a range of templates with preset styles and integrated CSS that are easy to use and customizable.[29]

CONTENTdm

This collection-management software organizes digital collections for group display and allows visitors the ability to search across holdings.[30] Though not a curated presentation of images, you may wish to provide cross-collection searching access for some virtual presentations.

Collective Access

Collective Access is an open source cataloging tool that allows you to grow robust digital records that can underpin your virtual sites.[31]

CollectionSpace

CollectionSpace is an open source, collections-management application with a suite of services for managing digital assets that can be used for online exhibition creation when customized.[32]

Open Exhibits

Open Exhibits is a tool kit you can use to create interactive components for web exhibits with digital assets, such as drag-and-drop features.[33]

Pachyderm

This open source multimedia authoring tool has pre-designed templates that play audio-video clips and allow for zooming functions that can enhance virtual exhibitions.[34]

Scalar

Branded as "born-digital, open source, media-rich scholarly publishing that's as easy as blogging," Scalar offers a free, open source platform for digital publishing that is highly flexible, customizable, and stocked with plug-ins to handle images and graphics.[35]

Definitions

- Accessibility—ability for a work to be understood, experienced, or appreciated by people despite disabilities
- Analytics—collection, analysis, and measurement of website data used to understand site use patterns and to enhance web use
- CSS—Cascading Style Sheets; web structures that format the layout of web pages and define size and text styles, promoting uniformity and building in accessibility features
- Digital exhibit—a virtual/web exhibition that showcases images, text, and perhaps audiovisual clips to educate, inspire, or celebrate a curated topic

Key Points

- You can develop web exhibitions in conjunction with physical exhibitions or create sites independent of a gallery experience
- Just as with physical exhibits, you develop and research virtual exhibits, letting broad learning objectives help you refine your narrative and item selection
- Being aware of barriers to use allows you to structure and create digital exhibitions that promote accessibility and improve user experience
- Virtual exhibits can be built from the ground up, from web exhibition–specific software, or developed in a hybrid model where existing coding structures are modified and tailored to your organization's needs

Notes

1. Reidsma, Matthew. 2014. *Responsive Web Design for Libraries: A LITA Guide.* Chicago: ALA TechSource, 65–67.

2. World Wide Web Consortium (W3C). 2008. "Web Content Accessibility Guidelines (WCAG) 2.0." Accessed September 1, 2020. https://www.w3.org/TR/WCAG20/.

3. Reidsma, Matthew. 2014. *Responsive Web Design for Libraries: A LITA Guide.* Chicago: ALA TechSource, 23–32.

4. Rush, Sharron. 2013. "Why Web Accessibility Matters for Cultural Institutions: Overview of Legal Requirements, Typical Problems, Practical Guidelines and Examples of Website Redesign." New York: Art Beyond Site. Accessed September 1, 2020. http://www.artbeyondsight.org/mei/white-papers-on-critical-issues-re-accessibility-and-inclusion/.

5. World Wide Web Consortium (W3C). 2008. "Web Content Accessibility Guidelines (WCAG) 2.0." Accessed September 1, 2020. https://www.w3.org/TR/WCAG20/.

6. Rush, Sharron. 2013. "Why Web Accessibility Matters for Cultural Institutions: Overview of Legal Requirements, Typical Problems, Practical Guidelines and Examples of Website Redesign." New York: Art Beyond Site. Accessed September 1, 2020. http://www.artbeyondsight.org/mei/wp-content/uploads/WP_MSWEB.pdf.

7. Rush, Sharron. 2013. "Why Web Accessibility Matters for Cultural Institutions: Overview of Legal Requirements, Typical Problems, Practical Guidelines and Examples of Website Redesign." New York: Art Beyond Site. Accessed September 1, 2020. http://www.artbeyondsight .org/mei/white-papers-on-critical-issues-re-accessibility-and-inclusion/.

8. Rush, Sharron. 2013. "Why Web Accessibility Matters for Cultural Institutions: Overview of Legal Requirements, Typical Problems, Practical Guidelines and Examples of Website Redesign." New York: Art Beyond Site. Accessed September 1, 2020. http://www.artbeyondsight .org/mei/white-papers-on-critical-issues-re-accessibility-and-inclusion/.

9. World Wide Web Consortium (W3C). 2008. "Web Content Accessibility Guidelines (WCAG) 2.0." Accessed September 1, 2020. https://www.w3.org/TR/WCAG20/.

10. Rush, Sharron. 2013. "Why Web Accessibility Matters for Cultural Institutions: Overview of Legal Requirements, Typical Problems, Practical Guidelines and Examples of Website Redesign." New York: Art Beyond Site. Accessed September 1, 2020. http://www.artbeyondsigh t.org/mei/white-papers-on-critical-issues-re-accessibility-and-inclusion/.

11. Rush, Sharron. 2013. "Why Web Accessibility Matters for Cultural Institutions: Overview of Legal Requirements, Typical Problems, Practical Guidelines and Examples of Website Redesign." New York: Art Beyond Site. Accessed September 1, 2020. http://www.artbeyondsight .org/mei/white-papers-on-critical-issues-re-accessibility-and-inclusion/.

12. World Wide Web Consortium (W3C). 2008. "Web Content Accessibility Guidelines (WCAG) 2.0." Accessed September 1, 2020. https://www.w3.org/TR/WCAG20/.

13. Rush, Sharron. 2013. "Why Web Accessibility Matters for Cultural Institutions: Overview of Legal Requirements, Typical Problems, Practical Guidelines and Examples of Website Redesign." New York: Art Beyond Site. Accessed September 1, 2020. http://www.artbeyondsight .org/mei/white-papers-on-critical-issues-re-accessibility-and-inclusion/.

14. Rush, Sharron. 2013. "Why Web Accessibility Matters for Cultural Institutions: Overview of Legal Requirements, Typical Problems, Practical Guidelines and Examples of Website Redesign." New York: Art Beyond Site. Accessed September 1, 2020. http://www.artbeyondsight .org/mei/white-papers-on-critical-issues-re-accessibility-and-inclusion/.

15. Duke University. "WCAG Principles and Guidelines." Accessed September 1, 2020. https://web.accessibility.duke.edu/learn/wcag-guidelines.

16. Stim, Richard. 2016. *Getting Permission: Using & Licensing Copyright-Protected Materials Online & Off.* Berkeley, CA: Nolo, 7.

17. Stim, Richard. 2016. *Getting Permission: Using & Licensing Copyright-Protected Materials Online & Off.* Berkeley, CA: Nolo, 7.

18. Stim, Richard. 2016. *Getting Permission: Using & Licensing Copyright-Protected Materials Online & Off.* Berkeley, CA: Nolo, 7–8.

19. Stim, Richard. 2016. *Getting Permission: Using & Licensing Copyright-Protected Materials Online & Off.* Berkeley, CA: Nolo, 10.

20. Stim, Richard. 2016. *Getting Permission: Using & Licensing Copyright-Protected Materials Online & Off.* Berkeley, CA: Nolo, 10–11.

21. Stim, Richard. 2016. *Getting Permission: Using & Licensing Copyright-Protected Materials Online & Off.* Berkeley, CA: Nolo, 256.

22. Stim, Richard. 2016. *Getting Permission: Using & Licensing Copyright-Protected Materials Online & Off.* Berkeley, CA: Nolo, 257.

23. Stim, Richard. 2016. *Getting Permission: Using & Licensing Copyright-Protected Materials Online & Off.* Berkeley, CA: Nolo, 256.

24. Stim, Richard. 2016. *Getting Permission: Using & Licensing Copyright-Protected Materials Online & Off.* Berkeley, CA: Nolo, 258.

25. Stim, Richard. 2016. *Getting Permission: Using & Licensing Copyright-Protected Materials Online & Off.* Berkeley, CA: Nolo, 257.

26. Stim, Richard. 2016. *Getting Permission: Using & Licensing Copyright-Protected Materials Online & Off.* Berkeley, CA: Nolo, 272.

27. Stim, Richard. 2016. *Getting Permission: Using & Licensing Copyright-Protected Materials Online & Off.* Berkeley, CA: Nolo, 274.

28. Open Education Database. "5 Free and Open Source Tools for Creating Web Exhibitions." Accessed September 1, 2020. https://oedb.org/ilibrarian/5-free-and-open-source-tools-for-creating-digital-exhibitions/.

29. Open Education Database. "5 Free and Open Source Tools for Creating Web Exhibitions." Accessed September 1, 2020. https://oedb.org/ilibrarian/5-free-and-open-source-tools-for-creating-digital-exhibitions/.

30. Open Education Database. "5 Free and Open Source Tools for Creating Web Exhibitions." Accessed September 1, 2020. https://oedb.org/ilibrarian/5-free-and-open-source-tools-for-creating-digital-exhibitions/.

31. Open Education Database. "5 Free and Open Source Tools for Creating Web Exhibitions." Accessed September 1, 2020. https://oedb.org/ilibrarian/5-free-and-open-source-tools-for-creating-digital-exhibitions/.

32. Open Education Database. "5 Free and Open Source Tools for Creating Web Exhibitions." Accessed September 1, 2020. https://oedb.org/ilibrarian/5-free-and-open-source-tools-for-creating-digital-exhibitions/.

33. Open Education Database. "5 Free and Open Source Tools for Creating Web Exhibitions." Accessed September 1, 2020. https://oedb.org/ilibrarian/5-free-and-open-source-tools-for-creating-digital-exhibitions/.

34. Open Education Database. "5 Free and Open Source Tools for Creating Web Exhibitions." Accessed September 1, 2020. https://oedb.org/ilibrarian/5-free-and-open-source-tools-for-creating-digital-exhibitions/.

35. Alliance for Networking Visual Culture. "About Scalar." Accessed September 1, 2020. https://scalar.me/anvc/.

References

Alliance for Networking Visual Culture. "About Scalar." Accessed September 1, 2020. https://scalar.me/anvc/.

Duke University. "WCAG Principles and Guidelines." Accessed September 1, 2020. https://web.accessibility.duke.edu/learn/wcag-guidelines.

Open Education Database. "5 Free and Open Source Tools for Creating Web Exhibitions." Accessed September 1, 2020. https://oedb.org/ilibrarian/5-free-and-open-source-tools-for-creating-digital-exhibitions/.

Reidsma, Matthew. 2014. *Responsive Web Design for Libraries: A LITA Guide.* Chicago: ALA TechSource.

Rush, Sharron. 2013. "Why Web Accessibility Matters for Cultural Institutions: Overview of Legal Requirements, Typical Problems, Practical Guidelines and Examples of Website Redesign." New York: Art Beyond Site. Accessed September 1, 2020. http://www.artbeyondsight.org/mei/wp-content/uploads/WP_MSWEB.pdf.

Stim, Richard. 2016. *Getting Permission: Using & Licensing Copyright-Protected Materials Online & Off.* Berkeley, CA: Nolo.

World Wide Web Consortium (W3C). 2008. "Web Content Accessibility Guidelines (WCAG) 2.0." Accessed September 1, 2020. https://www.w3.org/TR/WCAG20/.

Resources Mentioned in This Chapter

Accessibility Evaluator, WAVE: http://wave.webaim.org/

American Library Association's tools:

- Fair Use Evaluator: https://librarycopyright.net/resources/fairuse/index.php
- Public Domain Slider: https://librarycopyright.net/resources/digitalslider/index.html

Analytics: https://analytics.google.com
Color and Contrast Testers

- Coblis Color Blindness Simulator: https://www.color-blindness.com/coblis-color-blindness-simulator/
- WebAIM Contrast Checker: https://webaim.org/resources/contrastchecker/

Fair Use Image Sources

- Creative Commons Database: https://search.creativecommons.org/
- Flickr Creative Commons: https://www.flickr.com/creativecommons/
- Google Advanced Image Search (delimitate in the usage rights field): https://www.google.com/advanced_image_search
- Wikimedia Commons: https://commons.wikimedia.org/wiki/Main_Page

Open Source Tools

- Omeka: http://omeka.org/
- CONTENTdm: http://www.contentdm.org/
- Collective Access: http://collectiveaccess.org/
- CollectionSpace: http://www.collectionspace.org/
- Open Exhibits: http://openexhibits.org/
- Pachyderm: https://www.pachyderm.com/
- Scalar: https://scalar.me/anvc/

Readable: https://app.readable.com/text/
YouTube: https://www.youtube.com/

⑥ Further Reading

Crews, Kenneth D. 2012. *Copyright Law for Librarians and Educators: Creative Strategies and Practical Solutions*. Chicago: American Library Association.

Curtis, Donnelyn, ed. 2002. *Attracting, Educating, and Serving Remote Users through the Web: A How-to-Do-It Manual for Librarians, Number 114*. New York: Neal-Schuman Publishers.

Denzer, Juan. 2015. *Digital Collections and Exhibits*. Lanham, MD: Rowman & Littlefield.

Kalfatovic, Martin R. 2002. *Creating a Winning Online Exhibition: A Guide for Libraries, Archives, and Museums*. Chicago: American Library Association.

Reeb, Brenda. 2008. *Design Talk: Understanding the Roles of Usability, Practitioners, Web Designers, and Web Developers in User-Centered Web Design*. Chicago: Association of College and Research Libraries.

Thiel, Sarah Goodwin. 2007. *Build It Once: A Basic Primer for the Creation of Online Exhibitions*. Lanham, MD: Scarecrow Press.

Engage with It!

Programming and Interactives

What Is a Program?

A program is a plan or system with related activities toward a goal. It has a set start and end time for intended audiences. It usually requires a certain level of resource investment, including staffing, planning and preparation time, funding, space, and promotional needs. A program can take place in a physical space, virtual space, or a combination of both. The scale of a program can vary broadly from a one-on-one activity, to a large-scale or international event level depending on the resources invested. There is a wide spectrum of the types of programs, ranging from passive modes such as film screening, cooking demonstrations, lectures, panel discussions, to highly interactive and hands-on programs, such as book clubs, art- and craft-making activities, and food tasting events. A program can be a one-time, stand-alone experience, or serve as part of a larger series with multiple sessions that change content and rotate presenters. It can be indoors or outdoors on the library's premises, or out in the community. The format and the level of interactivity is determined based on many factors and considerations, including your library's strategic goals; administrative directions and guidelines; the availability of space, time, and budget; as well as the willingness and participation of key stakeholders.

Programming can boost your exhibit's success by helping you leverage your community networks. Exhibit programs provide entry points for your patrons to visit your exhibits and serve as the "hook" to get your patrons curious and excited about the different themes and stories your exhibits tell. Programs are fun and are excellent outreach tools to bring in both new and repeated users to the library. There are a number of benefits for patrons and the library.

Benefits for Patrons

Programs create and deepen connections with the subjects of the exhibitions. They shed light on elements that may or may not easily be identified in the exhibits, which can spark curiosity and conversation among patrons, and programs can create a space for people to forge strong bonds with friends and family.

Example

Culinary Curiosity was a collaborative exhibition that was made possible by Kendall College Trust and developed by the Arlington Heights Memorial Library, Aurora Public Library, Gail Borden Public Library District, and Schaumburg Township District Library. Conceived in 2006, the exhibit was developed specifically for the academic community of Kendall College of the National Louis University to showcase and support its culinary arts program. Due to acquisition and merger of the college and the facility in which the exhibit occupied, Kendall College Trust, the owner of *Culinary Curiosity*, needed to search for a new place to house the exhibit. Seeing the potential impact and strong connection to local history and culture, the four public libraries stepped in and joined forces to host the exhibit in 2019, making the exhibit accessible and open to the public for the first time. The libraries divided the 250 collection items among themselves and displayed them simultaneously.

Each library selected a section of the exhibit by comparing the themes of the collection to what resonated with their community's culture and history, as well as the partnership potential with their respective local businesses and organizations for programming. To maximize connectedness, the Aurora Public Library selected the themes of "Liquid Refreshments" and "Global Gastronomy" to pair with the presence of their city's beloved brewery, as well as to highlight their community's growing ethnic culinary diversity. The Gail Borden Public Library selected "Sweet Inventions and Bakers' Secrets" theme. A display of locally made cooking tools from the Elgin History Museum magnified the evolution of local businesses.

Each library developed their own suite of programs to amplify their respective themes. The Arlington Heights Memorial Library exhibits focused on the technological leap of cooking implements and food preparation methods. Their programs included "Pop-Up: Make a Cookie Jar," a drop-in event that engaged more than three hundred participants of every age, and "Chef Rose Bakes with Vegetables," which attracted nearly one hundred eager bakers. On the last day of the exhibit, a closing reception invited community members to see the exhibit a final time and to bring culinary items from their own families and kitchens for a special pop-up event. More than one hundred visitors came to the event and shared their personal items alongside the exhibit.

In addition to programs on-site, the libraries put together an online streamed event via Facebook Live. The event, "Catherine De Orio Talks Local Food," featured representatives from the four exhibiting libraries and the Executive Director of the Kendall College Trust in conversation with Catherine De Orio, former host of public television's *Check Please!*, a weekly television show that invites a rotating panel of three "citizen" reviewers to discuss local restaurants. More than thirty people attended the in-person event with the online segment reaching more than six thousand people. The program aimed to cross-promote library engagement and explore how the selected themes correlated and reflected culture and history in the respective communities.

Benefits for the Library

Talent Development

Developing and implementing programs require a high level of creativity, project management, and communication skills. The process of program development helps cultivate staff creativity and challenges them to expand on a given theme. Exhibit programming allows staff to experiment with alternative ideas; find resources, connections, and collaboration opportunities in hidden or unusual places; as well as predict the potential needs of the program recipients. These are valuable skills for librarians to possess and could be transferable to other areas of the library's operations.

Marketing Opportunity

As exhibits typically run for multiple weeks or months, programs refresh patrons' interest and keep the excitement going. You can schedule programs throughout the run of an exhibit. More than simply informing patrons about the exhibit, programs also promote the hosting library and its related services to individuals who might not be engaged otherwise.

⑥ Program Life Cycle

Program development sometimes takes on a life of its own. Depending on the available time, budget, personnel, and space, programs for exhibits can be small or large scale, in-house or off-site, interactive or passive. There are four main phases in a program development life cycle: staying informed, formulation, implementation, and evaluation.

Phase 1: Staying Informed

A time-saving way in developing programs for any exhibit is to stay informed about current trends and interests in your community, as well as available resources in your area. Subscribe to newsletters and listservs of relevant organizations, such as other libraries, museums, cultural institutions, special event venues, associations, special interest groups, book clubs, research companies, and blogs. Share and discuss interesting and relevant information with your team or individuals who might be involved in the exhibit planning. If time and budget permits, consider attending the events and experience them firsthand as part of ongoing professional development. This practice allows librarians to

Example: *Above and Beyond* at the Harold Washington Library Center of the Chicago Public Library, 2016–2020

This art exhibit commemorated the courage and sacrifice of American soldiers in the Vietnam War and offered special viewings with veteran docents (see figure 8.1). Audiences could talk to the docents about their personal experiences during programs held over the Memorial Day weekend in 2017. The library organized a book reading event with live music with contributors of *I Remember: Chicago Veterans of War*. The library promoted the program through its newsletter and website, as well as via local news and the veteran community network in the Chicago metropolitan area.[1]

Figure 8.1. Installation view of *Above and Beyond* exhibit at the Harold Washington Library Center of the Chicago Public Library. *Patti Gibbons.*

put themselves in the shoes of a program attendee and critically reflect on the operations of the program.

Phase 2: Formulation

This is the stage where you develop the specifics of your program as informed by the information you have gathered. You are now "giving life" to the program by setting the perimeter, including your objective, the budget, staffing needs, potential partnerships, and the schedule.

Setting an Objective

Once the exhibit is approved or confirmed, identify what you want to achieve in your programs. As stated, there is great value in developing and hosting programs in conjunction with your exhibit, but be careful not to fall into autopilot mode and run programs without thinking critically about why you do it, how they can be relevant and meaningful to your audience, and whether your library can practically support the programs given the time, space, budget, and staff available.

Determining Funding Availability and Making a Budget

As you start planning your overall exhibit, estimate the number of programs you will want to include. In libraries with restricted funding, identify the potential of sponsorship, grant opportunities, or in-kind donation for any exhibit and associated programming. Outside support helps stretch budgets and offers unique and desirable opportunities to engage external partners.

Once you have your annual exhibit budget that includes programming, there are several factors to consider as you develop an exhibit-specific program budget:

- How many programs do we want to have during the run of the exhibit?
- What types of programs will we have? Are these self-directed, hands-on, or lecture-based programs?
- Who will facilitate the programs? Staff or outside presenters? If outside presenters, what honorariums can my library afford?
- What additional supplies and materials does each program need? Can the cost be shared with other departments, or external partners?
- Where will the programs take place? At the library or off-site? If off-site, will there be a rental fee?
- When in the run of the exhibit will the program be offered? How might this impact costs?
- Is the program free or charged? If charged, what are the price points?
- Do we have contingency funding for the programs?

Getting Staff

Get your allies. As the budget is approved, gather a group of creative minds and talents to generate ideas for programming. These people may or may not continue to actually handle the logistics of delivering and hosting the programs, but can serve as advisors or a sounding board. Their insights will be particularly useful in making sure the programs are in line with the interest of your library's users.

When your programs require additional staffing that may be beyond the capacity of your current paid staff, consider recruiting volunteers. Engaging volunteers in your exhibit program can be fun, meaningful, and perhaps life changing to some. Building and maintaining an effective infrastructure to support a volunteer program helps extend the reach of the library exhibit. Volunteers can play a significant role, helping your library achieve many exhibit goals. Volunteers act as the ambassadors and advocates for your exhibit and can be the perfect influencer for your word-of-mouth marketing (see chapter 9).

Library exhibit docents lead guided tours and provide patrons with insights into exhibits that deepen the experience. In kids-oriented, interactive exhibits, volunteers facilitate art activities for children and their caregivers. Volunteers are instrumental in maintaining exhibit tidiness, especially when staffing is short. To record and capture information about visitor engagement in the exhibit, volunteer surveyors help conduct direct observation and data collecting in exhibits. During summers, teen volunteers provide additional administrative support and gain workplace and specific job skills and credentials, while building their social network.

As you plan your exhibit and its associated programming, think about ways to effectively use volunteers. Some areas to consider include the following:

- Identify your volunteer needs and qualification requirements

  ○ What type of volunteer support do we need?
  ○ What job title best reflects the role?
  ○ How many volunteers do we need?
  ○ What qualifications are necessary to perform the job?

  Once you answer these questions, draft a job description that includes the expected duration of the position, service hours, and, for teen volunteers, whether the hours can be put toward their community service credit for school. If your library can provide the credits for teen volunteers, before launch, be sure to check with corresponding institutions for proper paperwork.

- Develop recruitment and placement strategies

  ○ Where can we find prospective volunteers?
  ○ Who should be the best point person to answer the inquiries at my library?
  ○ Are we willing and/or ready to pay for posting the volunteer job ad?
  ○ How do we determine the placement of volunteers for the greatest benefits of the exhibit?

  Draft an announcement that could go to listservs, websites, social networking platforms, or even create a flyer or poster for distribution. Consider sharing this with other departments or making an announcement during other library programs where you may attract candidates. And just as with paid positions, consider whether a formal interview is needed.

- Onboarding

  ○ What policies and procedures do volunteers need to know about?
  ○ If there are no policies or procedures, who should volunteers consult for guidance?

  This step can be taken as soon as the volunteer accepts the offer or, to keep their memory fresh, closer to the time when the position begins.

- Design training that covers both subject contents and specific skills relevant to the volunteer position

  ○ For positions that require more advanced skills, consider what materials the volunteers need to be familiar with
  ○ How long will the training be?
  ○ Will you need to pull in other staff members to run it?
  ○ When is the best day or time to run the training?

- Service hours documentation

  ○ How will you keep track of the volunteers' service hours?
  ○ Will they be required to "clock in/out" and how important is the data for your library?
  ○ What would be the most efficient way to track volunteer hours?

  Many libraries use fee-based software, such as Volgistics, for tracking the hours. If volunteer management is already part of your library's operations, this expense may originate outside the exhibit programming budget. If the exhibit volunteer program is a new venture, discuss with your administration whether or not the expense is worthwhile for the exhibit.

- Performance monitoring and quality assurance

  ○ How will you measure whether volunteers are succeeding in the position?
  ○ Who should conduct the evaluation?

  It is best to encourage excellence in work performance, just as for paid positions. Be sure to communicate the expectation to the volunteers during onboarding and training and establish mutual understanding early on.

- Service acknowledgment and celebration

  When the volunteers complete their service, be ready to acknowledge and celebrate it. Make it an experience that your library community remembers. As your library continues planning exhibits in the future, take this as an opportunity to build camaraderie.

Finding Partners

In the process of staff brainstorming and discussion, keep in mind what partnership opportunities are available. Partnerships can be internal, cross-department, or external. Partnerships in the context of programming are typically focused on sharing resources. Resources may include but are not limited to sponsorships, venue hosting, event marketing, or volunteer program support, and partnership can possibly include co-curating an exhibit or co-authoring the text that accompanies the exhibit. The date, time, and other specifics of the program can be co-determined based on the partner's availability and schedule.

Scheduling

While different organizations have different approaches to program scheduling, there are common concerns that libraries must take into consideration:

- Typical visitor pattern: Track door counts that can be broken down by hours, days, weeks, and months. Data collection and analysis on the time of the day and day of the week allows library staff an insight into the popular time slots and seasons to maximize visitor attendance and the impact of the program.
- Visitor feedback: As you gather your staff on the advisory team, ask about anecdotal comments on certain types of programs that have been running. Direct interaction with customers helps the library learn about visitor preferences.
- Religious observance, cultural holidays, and community calendars: Acknowledge, respect, and honor dates that are important to your community. Seek opportunities to celebrate with your community through partnerships. You may take a pause on holding any events on and around those dates.
- Space availability: If space is a limitation at your library or if it is shared with the public or other entities, watch for any similar programming that has been booked. Prioritize the exhibit programs based on its availability.
- Transportation and parking availability: Surrounding amenities can be something easily overlooked when it comes to program scheduling. Consider the convenience, accessibility, and availability of public transportation and parking at your potential program time.
- Check surrounding institutions' schedules for conflicts: Are your "competitors" doing any major events during that time?

The bottom line is: Think from your audience's point of view from the start to the end of the program to encourage and enable participation.

Contracting

If you partner with outside presenters or agencies, regardless of whether it involves a monetary commitment, have a contract prepared that details all the specifications, such as the program date, time, location where the program will be held, program description, name and contact information of the presenter or representation of the agency, program registration, and the responsibilities and expectations of both parties. Information about photo and/or content release should be included along with any credit line wording, especially if you use materials for promotional use. You should also be explicit about your cancellation policy and liability statements. If payment for the presenter is involved, note the amount, payment schedule, delivery method, and any additional document requirement for the payment in the contract. The contract should be signed by a library representative and the presenter, and each keeps a countersigned copy.

If drafting a contract is new to you, the best way is to work with your financial department to make sure the terms are clear and in compliance with the library's policies and

WHY DIVERSITY, EQUITY, AND INCLUSION MATTER IN YOUR PROGRAMMING

Don't just make any program, make one that embraces diversity, equity, and inclusion, and make these ideas clear and loud to your audience. These are the questions you should ask yourself as you plan your exhibit programs:

- Does the physical environment in which the program is held makes people feel welcomed and valued?
- If the physical space has limitations, consider what alternative solutions you can provide to ensure your audience feels welcomed and included. For example, for guests with hearing impairment who are attending a lecture or panel discussion, offer an option for them to use assistive listening devices. For visitors with limited English proficiency, consider programs conducted in other languages or provide translation in print during the program.
- Does your program timing suit your target audience's needs?
- Is your program topic and/or description written in a way that may evoke any negative connotation or offend any group in your community?
- Is the focus of the program reflective of your patrons' current interests and needs?
- Is your expected audience size too big or too small for your patrons to be able to fully engage?

This is not a comprehensive list, but it is a starting point of things to consider to be sensitive to and anticipate the various needs of your patrons.

procedures. If you have an existing contract, be sure to review and update it as necessary. Allow adequate time for multiple reviews before finalizing and using it. Sometimes, the presenter may bring their own contract. Here, check with your finance department to determine if their contract is acceptable in lieu of the library's version. Keep the signed copies and secure them for future reference, particularly if you are interested in bringing back the presenter.

Phase 3: Implementation

Once all pieces are in place, you are ready to roll out your program. Be sure to have constant and clear communication with staff and volunteers to make sure they understand the logistics of the exhibit and program and are able to answer potential inquiries from your library visitors. Create talking points and share with other staff to avoid potential confusion.

Phase 4: Evaluation

Consider what evidence you would like to collect to evaluate your program. For traveling exhibits especially, it is customary, and in some cases required, to document exhibit programs and activities as a way to demonstrate visitor engagement and impact. Your documentation may include the following:

- Photos and video recordings of visitors interacting in your program—and be sure to be upfront about photo permission
- Quotes from your audience
- Evidence of press coverage, such as newspaper clippings, external blog posts, reviews, other links
- Program attendance data
- Exit survey responses

As mentioned, goal setting is vital to the success of exhibit programming (and anything else). Evaluation for exhibits or informal learning environments is a broad topic, and we will discuss evaluation more in-depth in chapter 10.

⊚ Interactive Opportunities

Beyond developing programs that are run at a set time, consider hands-on activities, or gallery interactives, that can enhance visitor engagement with an exhibit. There are three common types of interactives in libraries: digital kiosks, hands-on activities, and takeaways.

Digital Kiosks

Digital tablets offer an easy way to create kiosks that display digital files from your library collections and archives. Kiosk Pro is a commonly used and flexible kiosk browser app for iOS and iPad OS. It displays interactive content like HTML pages, PDFs, and videos. Hardware is also available for purchase to create fully customized tablet kiosks specifically for exhibit use. For libraries that are interested in gathering more targeted feedback on the exhibit, the kiosks can serve as a survey platform to measure the exhibit impact. (See figure 8.2.)

Hands-On Activities

Interactive components in exhibits help address different learning styles. Low-tech activities, such as coloring, writing, drawing, model building, button making, and other making projects can be great entry points for diverse audiences to achieve the same learning objectives. Through experiential learning, movements, and reflections, "makerspaces" help visitors strengthen their connections to specific topics in the exhibit. These activities can take place as an ongoing part of the exhibit or in pop-up fashion.

Takeaways

Supplementary takeaways can be effective, low-cost ways to allow visitors to extend their learning from the exhibit. Some takeaways are also part of hands-on activities in exhibits. For example, you can provide coloring pages with images related to the exhibit theme or

Figure 8.2. Installation view of *#beinthecircle* exhibit at Arlington Heights Memorial Library. *Carol Ng-He.*

This section is contributed by Juan Denzer, Engineering and Computer Science Librarian, Syracuse University Library, and author of *Digital Collections and Exhibits.*

Adding technology to exhibits can be easy to implement, inexpensive, and reusable. Here are a few examples of technology that will add sight, sound, and touch to your exhibits without ruining your budget.

Adding Touch and Sound with Bare Conductive Touch Board

Imagine being able to add that user experience to your exhibit without having to make complicated wire connections and write any code. If you can use a paint-brush, twist wire, and copy files to a memory card, then you can add that great experience to your exhibit.

Programmable microcontroller boards are great for all types of do-it-yourself projects. One of the most popular open source boards is the Arduino. There are many types of Arduino boards and many companies have developed their own based on the Arduino. One company is Bare Conductive. They created a board called the Bare Conductive Touch Board. The board allows you to add capacitive and proximity touch to any project. It can be used to play sounds or turn on/off LEDs. It can even be programmed to control more advanced things such as servos and solenoids. The board has all of that built into one circuit board, and the best part is that you can start using it right out of the box—without having to write any computer code or upload the code to the board. The code is already pre-programmed. All that is needed is to copy audio files in the form of MP3s to an SD memory card.

Making the board touch interactive is just as easy. The board can become touch interactive by connecting a conductive wire or using conductive paint, which can be behind a picture or added to an object. The proximity sensor is sensitive enough so that you don't even have to touch the object. This can be part of a music exhibit from your collection. There are plenty of sample projects that come with how-to instructions and the code—everything from creating a proximity wall sensor to how-to-send data via Bluetooth with a touch board.

Using Virtual Green Screen with an Xbox Kinect

Between 2010 and 2017, Microsoft released various versions of Kinects for the Xbox 360 gaming system. The first version was designed to add real-time gesture recognition for video gamers to play virtual games, such as baseball, bowling, and rafting, without a controller or any wearable device. Later, the product was rebranded as Kinect for Windows, and an accompanying software development kit (SDK) was released to allow users to hack the Kinect and create custom software. The Kinect SDK for Windows not only tapped into the power of gesture recognition, it also opened up the 3D depth capabilities of the Kinect, allowing for other exciting video effects such as a green screen. There are four types of Kinects based on the Xbox gaming system:

- Kinect for Xbox 360 (2010)
- Kinect for Windows V1 (2012)
- Kinect for Xbox One (2013)
- Kinect for Windows V2 (2014)

Adding the Kinect to an exhibit is as easy as plugging in the device, installing the SDK, and running a program. If you are using the Kinect for Windows, you will have much more compatibility, which makes the Kinect green screen work better. For instance, the Xbox 360 will have trouble recognizing multiple people, whereas the Kinect for Windows can handle more people on a green screen. The costs for the Kinects vary depending on the version.

What makes the Kinect a better choice than a regular webcam with an actual green screen is that it does not require a physical green screen. You can achieve the same effect without having to set up a one-color screen background. The Kinect can be placed almost anywhere with good lighting. You can create a space that complements your exhibit without having a distracting blank screen in the background. The Kinect also allows you to create the green screen effect in real time. Unlike other systems, there is no need to render any images after a photo is taken. You can take screenshots by simply pressing a button. You can even add a second display and have users move around on the green screen.

Although Microsoft stopped production of the Kinect in 2017, you can still get code for them on GitHub, which is an open source repository where people share code. Additionally, Microsoft released a new version of Kinect called the Azure Kinect, which is based on the original Kinect and redesigned to be completely open source, allowing for a cloud-based service. For this reason, you can make use of artificial intelligence (AI) and machine learning to create even more exciting uses for exhibits. You can create a pop-up studio that is rendered in the blink of an eye. The new Kinect can be combined with AR and VR headsets to create an even more immersive experience for users. With its strong open source support from Microsoft and a growing community of developers, the Kinect will bring some exciting uses for libraries to incorporate into their exhibits.

story; a scavenger hunt worksheet that features selected items, artifacts, or characters in your exhibit; and booklists or resource guides.

Off-Site/Outreach Activities

Exhibit programming does not have to occur within the confines of the library. You can partner with others to extend your reach. By bringing exhibit programs to the community and co-creating with community members and partners, libraries enhance accessibility and expand the audience base.

Example 1: *XOXO: An Exhibition about Love and Forgiveness* at Arlington Heights Memorial Library

To further engage the community in actively sharing love and kindness during the *XOXO: An Exhibition about Love and Forgiveness*, the library developed two outreach programs. First, the library partnered with the Wheeling Township Food Pantry on a community food drive to collect donations of their most needed food items. Second, the library partnered with Girls Love Mail, a national initiative that sends handwritten letters of support to women newly diagnosed with breast cancer. Exhibit visitors at the library and residents off-site at a senior center reading room wrote letters.

Example 2: *Earl B. Dickerson* exhibit, D'Angelo Law Library at the University of Chicago

The D'Angelo Law School created an exhibit to celebrate the centennial of the graduation of one of their most distinguished alumnus, Earl B. Dickerson. A group of historians and legal scholars hosted a two-day conference with the first day focusing on the life and accomplishments of Dickerson in historical perspective and the second day engaging Chicago lawyers and activists through a series of discussions and performances.

⊚ Definitions

- Diversity—a belief and practice of accepting and embracing differences among people; characteristics and attributes such as race, ethnicity, gender, sexual orientation, age, religion, socioeconomic status, occupation, community affiliation, education level, marital status, language, abilities, physical appearance, as well as values and perspectives are considered
- Equity—a treatment that acknowledges individual circumstance, eliminates unnecessary barriers that have prevented certain groups from fully participating, and provides resources to people according to their individual circumstance and need so that they can gain access to opportunities
- Inclusion—a way of thinking and effort to create a bias-free culture or environment in which people feel valued, supported, and welcomed as they are
- Program—a plan or project with related activities toward a goal

⊚ Key Points

- Exhibit programming benefits patrons and the library in many ways
- Program life cycle involves four phases, including staying informed, formulation, implementation, and evaluation
- Three common gallery interactives are digital kiosks, hands-on activities, and takeaways

- Off-site or outreach activities can be done through collaboration with external organizations

◎ Note

1. *eNews Park Forest.* 2017. "National Veterans Art Museum Announces Events in Honor of Memorial Day 2017." Accessed September 1, 2020. https://www.enewspf.com/opinion/blog-posts/national-veterans-art-museum-announces-events-honor-memorial-day-2017/.

◎ References

eNews Park Forest. 2017. "National Veterans Art Museum Announces Events in Honor of Memorial Day 2017." Accessed September 1, 2020. https://www.enewspf.com/opinion/blog-posts/national-veterans-art-museum-announces-events-honor-memorial-day-2017/.

Resources Mentioned in This Chapter

Azure Kinect: https://azure.microsoft.com/en-us/services/kinect-dk/
Bare Conductive: https://www.bareconductive.com/resources
GitHub: https://github.com/
Kiosk Pro: https://www.kioskgroup.com/pages/kiosk-pro-software
Volgistics: https://www.volgistics.com/

◎ Further Reading

Bombaro, Christine. 2020. *Diversity, Equity, and Inclusion in Action: Planning, Leadership and Programming.* Atlanta, GA: ALA Editions.

Demeter, Michelle, and Holmes, Haley K. 2019. *Library Programming Made Easy: A Practical Guide for Librarians.* Lanham, MD: Rowman & Littlefield.

Denzer, Juan. 2015. *Digital Collections and Exhibits.* Lanham, MD: Rowman & Littlefield.

Vatsky, Sharon. 2018. *Museum Gallery Activities: A Handbook.* Arlington, VA: American Alliance of Museums.

Market It!

Publicity and Promotion

YOU HAVE PUT A LOT OF ENERGY, time, and resources into making exhibits happen. You will want to let your community know about the work so they can visit the exhibit and participate in your programs. Marketing can help you reach audiences and help ensure your exhibit is meeting its set goals. Using a variety of marketing strategies—including social media channels, online marketing, target marketing, promotional materials, partnerships, and word of mouth, you can invite your target audience to participate in your library exhibits. There are a great variety of marketing resources available for library professionals. This chapter provides a specific framework for promoting exhibits and displays.

◎ Marketing Stages

Marketing is more than just identifying promotional channels. It is a strategy to add value to the communities your library serves and ties directly to your library's mission. "Marketing and outreach efforts extend to both internal and external markets including staff, administrators, legislators, collaborators, media outlets, and funding agencies."[1]

Your marketing should start before the exhibit opens. It is key to building anticipation and excitement, by making your community aware of the exhibit and piquing their curiosity. There are four key marketing stages:

- Research and framing
- Pre-exhibit marketing
- Exhibit launch
- Post-exhibit marketing

Research and Framing

Creating an exhibit takes time and research to build an impactful and meaningful experience that resonates with your audience. Before you start actively promoting your exhibit, it is important to think about how you will plan your marketing strategy. The first step is to get a clear understanding of the goals of your exhibit. Exhibit goals should support your organization's larger strategic goals, but also flexibly respond to your community's current social and cultural needs.

Then, identify the segment of your community you want to target with your marketing efforts and select the appropriate outlets that correlate to your target audience's interests and preferences. Conduct an environmental scan to gather information on the latest research studies on marketing, review secondary sources about your community and discuss them with your team, and track demographic data and trends that can guide your exhibit marketing plan. This information helps you benchmark library exhibits.

Next, develop a budget for your marketing activity. You may have to consult with your administration in order to create an appropriate budget. Focus your conversations with your organizational leadership on how your exhibit will address organizational goals, supported by well-researched information. Use inspirational examples from peer organizations that have done similar work so that you can help your organization to make informed decisions.

An environmental scan is an analysis that gathers data about the community to assist in planning with a purpose.

—SUSAN W. ALMAN

Once you determine your marketing budget, assign roles and responsibilities to people. If your library has a marketing team, work with them to develop messaging about the exhibit, ways to reach different segments of your community; start identifying promotional channels and setting the priority and timeline of your marketing activities. It is always helpful to share this information so there will be no overlaps or surprises along the way. If you don't have a marketing team to work with, set up informal conversations with peers outside of your library to get insights and learn from their experiences, or even create an interest group through appropriate professional networks to gather advice.

At this stage, if it is an in-house exhibit project, this is the time to develop branding. For traveling exhibits, lending organizations provide their branding guidelines. Branding reinforces the public impression about the exhibit and allows for more consistent messaging.

Branding captures your exhibit's big ideas and articulates the "look" and "feel" that best convey its central themes. Don't be shy: make a long list then narrow from there. If your marketing team is small, consider soliciting ideas from colleagues at your library who develop programs that sometimes take the similar creative route for their pitch. They can be an excellent sounding board for you. Alternatively, finding inspiration from museum exhibition websites and their promotional outlets can be a great method for your research.

Pre-Exhibit Marketing

Following the research and framing stage is pre-exhibit marketing, which focuses on creating awareness, building anticipation, and piquing general interest before the exhibit formally opens. Marketing approaches used in this stage of the marketing plan include press releases and a newsletter, as well as creating a website for the exhibit. When it gets close to the exhibit opening date, you may also want to start using social media.

Exhibit Launch

Promotion doesn't stop once the exhibit is up and running. After the exhibit launches, marketing should focus on maximizing its reach and drawing attendance. Social media platforms are an excellent tool during this stage of the marketing process. Social media will enable you to share anecdotal exhibit feedback and reactions, which could entice more interest from people who have not seen the exhibit. In addition, physical promotional materials are critical to spread the word about the exhibit in a tangible way. For instance, in-house signage guides people who happen to stumble upon the exhibit without having received any advance communication.

Post-Exhibit Marketing

Marketing doesn't stop once the exhibit is over. Newsletters, blogs, and social media posts are typically used at this stage to share the impact of your exhibit and highlight visitor experiences. This also helps raise the organization's overall profile and maintain the connectivity with your community. This phase offers an opportunity for reflection on the success of the exhibit and your marketing plans. For future reference, gather all media and press coverage and run a publicity report to capture the marketing activities and public impressions about your exhibit.

Promotional Channels

Once you have a marketing strategy in place, you can start to think about which specific promotional channels will help you reach your desired target audience. Depending on your exhibit budget, you may be able to employ all or some of the promotional ideas described here. In the end, through careful research, analysis, planning, and monitoring of your chosen marketing activities, you have to be willing to proactively seek out marketing opportunities that align with your exhibit goals and make sense to your target audience.

Target Marketing

Target market refers to a segment of potential exhibit visitors or patrons your library intends to promote to and engage with. We start with the traditional methods, as they are time-tested. They also provide a solid base of content that you can use in other emerging and digital methods.

Media List

A media list documents the key media contacts who would be interested in the stories about your exhibits and library. The list includes contact information for individuals or groups that will promote your library and exhibits through news outlets. You can keep this as a simple spreadsheet for easy sorting. Note the preferences of ways, format, and timeframe organizations prefer receiving the information. Always keep this list up-to-date to make your effort effective.[2]

One way to start developing your media list is to identify potential partners in your community, industry, and niche groups that have connections with the topics in your exhibit. For example:

- For university libraries: include academic departments, campus museums, the alumni relations department, campus and student life departments, and communications and external relations departments
- For public libraries: list local businesses, local media outlets, farmers' markets, and schools
- For museum or special libraries: note nearby university and school libraries

You can share exhibit announcements, press releases, and other promotional materials with these partners to have them help spread the word to their communities.

Press Releases

A press release is a 300- to 400-word document that follows a standard format. It generally includes your organization's letterhead or logo, media contact information, headline, release date, introduction, body, and a boilerplate that gives the general information about your organization. Press releases aim to promote something significant and specific, such as the purpose of your exhibit, featured exhibit components, related special events or programs and their target audience, and quotes from your administrator, exhibit organizer, or patrons. The recipients of your press release are wide-ranging, such as community partners, local news stations, and library consortia (if they have a news section on their website and other promotional platforms).

Newsletter

A newsletter is a traditional and time-honored way for libraries to communicate with their communities. It can be either print or electronic. If your organization already has a newsletter, consider the scale and placement of the exhibit information along with other events and resources. Since some exhibits run for more than a month, think about how you want to lay out and unfold the story about your exhibit. In addition to your regular newsletter, you may also want to create an additional electronic newsletter dedicated to just exhibits. This will enable you to connect with different audiences than your organization's regular newsletter typically reaches. Affordable newsletter management applications are listed at the end of this chapter.

Promotional Materials

Promotional materials are giveaway items for a wide range of audiences. They typically come in two formats: print and "swag." Printed materials include banners, newsletters, pamphlets, posters, flyers, and stickers. They can be distributed at the service points inside the library or off-site during school visits or other community programs. To promote *XOXO: An Exhibit about Love and Forgiveness*, the Arlington Heights Memorial Library incorporated print-based promotional materials into its marketing strategy. Using its lender's branding, the library designed and gave away heart-shaped stickers that had the library's name and the showtimes for the exhibit. Swag items include branded products such as stationery and book bags. Be creative with your exhibit swag. Think about the relevance to your exhibit theme, usefulness, appropriateness to diverse audiences, and affordability as you brainstorm about types of promotional materials for exhibits. The four public libraries that collaborated to launch individual parts of the multi-venue collaborative *Culinary Curiosity* exhibit each branded a different product with their own logo as an incentive for visitors to collect the set and visit all four locations. The Arlington Heights Memorial Library gave out measuring spoons and the Schaumburg Township District Library offered chip bag clips.

Word of Mouth

Word of mouth is a great marketing tool because it enables authentic sharing of first-person experiences, which helps to build the reputation of your exhibit and organization. Good word of mouth doesn't occur without help. Create opportunities for your visitors to spread the word. Start by thinking back to who your target market is and identify their preferences. Often, programming and marketing go hand in hand, and creating exclusive access to your exhibits could be one way to attract your target market and spread the word through them. By crafting exclusive engagements with your audience, you amplify how unique the experience can be. Later, we will talk about the use of social media outlets; they are also effective tools to build your word-of-mouth marketing

> We think WOMM [word-of-mouth marketing] makes sense for libraries for three very good reasons. One, because we can afford it. For the first time, the playing field is level. We can compete. We can win public awareness and support. Two, libraries have a potential sales force of millions, including our entire staff, friends, trustees, and satisfied customers who for the most part we have not tapped. And three, because it absolutely is the most powerful form of communication.[3]

Online Marketing

Web pages can offer many possibilities for exhibits. As discussed in chapter 7, not only can a web page serve as a repository of information about the exhibit, it can also be the platform for the exhibit itself. It is a highly effective marketing tool. When thinking about the exhibit's website as a marketing tool, tips to note include these:

- Sync website content with your social media feeds because cross-promotion enhances the visibility of your exhibit posts

- Make your exhibit website easy to find. If it is a micro-site of your organization's website, be sure to place it in a prominent location that can be accessed with a few clicks.
- To make your site engaging, go beyond written descriptions about the exhibit and incorporate videos, images, testimonials, stories, and resources
- Use your librarian powers and link your website to your database or search catalog to encourage extended learning for your users. Create LibGuides for diverse audiences on various themes from your exhibit.
- Incorporate a blog. Blogs are generally less formal and structured then websites, and they provide more in-depth insights about the specific aspect of the exhibits. Keep blog content dynamic by using multiple bloggers to diversify the voices in your blog.

Social Media Channels

Social media has become an integral part of many organizations' overall marketing strategies. According to a 2019 study by the Pew Research Center, Facebook, YouTube, and Instagram are the most widely used online platforms among adults ages eighteen or older in the United States.[4] It is important for library professionals to keep up with the marketing trends. Understanding the features and social engagement capabilities social media platforms offer in terms of marketing can help you reach new audiences. Be bold in experimenting with new ways of staying social with your community and find ways to collaborate internally or with other libraries and content providers to advance your marketing endeavors.

> But when all is said and done, predicting the future of any kind of technology is nigh impossible, says Keren Mills, digital services development officer, library services, at the Open University of the United Kingdom. . . . "Collaboration between libraries or consortiums and content providers is growing in importance for enabling both types of organization to innovate fast enough to keep up with increasingly rapid changes in technology and user expectations."[5]

As you explore the marketing possibilities of various social media platforms, consider the populations each platform caters to and the unique features available. However, the following are some rules of thumbs in using social media for exhibit promotional campaigns regardless of the specific platform you use.

Set Goals

Align your goals for marketing via social media with your goals for the exhibit and your organization. Be SMART (Specific, Measurable, Attainable, Realistic, and Timely) in planning your posts and developing the content. For example, use consistent language and wording in your marketing efforts. Set your target number of views or reactions you would like to see for a specific post and make sure the number is set using evidence-based research or industry benchmarks. The campaign of posts should be implemented and tracked regularly or in the expected timeframe.

Create Branded Images

Create a branded image of your exhibit, including the title, tagline (if available), dates of the exhibit run, and links for more details. Use these images on all your social media platforms to create a cohesive message.

Show Up Often

Make a schedule of when you will post. The old saying, "Out of sight, out of mind," is true—especially with fast-moving social media feeds. The Pew Research Institute's study reveals that roughly three-quarters of Facebook users (74 percent) visit the site daily, including about half who do so several times a day.[6] Regular postings are key to staying engaged with your community. Strike a balance with other programs, services, and initiatives of your organizations in planning your schedule.

Be Concise

When planning your posts, think from the readers' point of view and avoid long posts that people have to scroll to finish. This is especially true as the use of mobile apps is on the rise. Limit your word count and use engaging visuals, such as pictures or infographics, to boost reactions and initiate comments (see figure 9.1).

Incorporate Your Social Media Handle

Cross-promote your organization's social media handles with all your exhibit's promotional materials (see figure 9.2). This will make it easy for your target audience to find and share information about the exhibit.

Be Creative

Go beyond just the basics about the exhibit. Consider incorporating a variety of visuals, such as close-up photos of specific items on display or of exhibit programs, or a snapshot showing the full view of the installation. Take your followers behind the scenes into the process of your exhibit planning, production, and installation. Showcase staff members whose roles are not public facing, such as conservators, graphic designers, or facilities crew, to talk about their contributions in the exhibit.

Engage a Social Media Influencer

Consider collaborating with a local social media influencer. Social media influencers are defined as "people who have built a reputation for their knowledge and expertise on a specific topic. They make regular posts about that topic on their preferred social media channels and generate large followings of enthusiastic, engaged people who pay close attention to their views."[7] For your exhibit promotion, identify these individuals. Have a conversation with them about your exhibit and how their participation can contribute to your goals and impact your community positively, and then invite them to partner with your organization. You might consider having an influencer "take over" your organization's social media feed and allowing them to create posts in your organization's account. To tap into communities that either party might not be able to do otherwise could be a

Figure 9.1. Instagram post. *Los Angeles Public Library.*

Figure 9.2. Instagram post. *New York Public Library.*

win-win situation for both the influencer and your organization. Engaging an influencer helps increase publicity, at little or no financial commitment on the library's part, while enhancing moral support to your organization.

Make Videos

Videos have gained popularity in the last few years on all social media platforms. Videos can be captivating and they can also put a human face to the exhibit and the organization as a whole. Here are a few ideas for exhibit-related videos:

- Tell a story. People love stories and a narrative will enable you to use video to its fullest potential.
- Conduct an interview with a social media influencer during the exhibit and invite them to share their reflections and connections with an object or story in the exhibit. These testimonials are persuasive and can move viewers toward an action.
- Reveal interesting or the behind-the-scenes aspects of the exhibition
- Give a virtual exhibit tour to highlight what is included in the exhibit
- If possible, collaborate with your digital services or IT department to make use of their skills and expertise
- Include your organization's logo or branding at the beginning and the end of the video

- Try to keep your videos under two minutes
- Include a detailed description about the video and provide a link to your organization

#usehashtags

Hashtags are a convenient way for visitors to share and search for the topic relating to your exhibit. *Hashtags*, words or phrases preceded by a hash sign (#), are used on social media websites and applications to identify related messages and are easily searchable by specific topics. They are particularly prevalent on Twitter because of its word limit. Hashtags enable users to search specific topics across an entire social media platform. If your organization does not have a hashtag, create one as your brand and use it consistently not just for exhibits but other events as well. Reviewing how your hashtag is used by visitors could help your organization evaluate the success of the marketing strategy during the post-exhibit marketing phase.

Use Analytics to Time Your Post

Most social media platforms provide analytics that show which type of content gets the most clicks and impressions. Use the data wisely to plan your promotional strategy and ensure you are posting marketing materials at times when you know your target audience will be most likely to engage.

Be Responsive

A key aspect of all successful social media–based marketing is prompt responses to comments. Turn on notifications to receive immediate alerts of comments. It reflects your care for your followers and shows your interest in engaging with your community.

Livestream or Live Tweet Your Events

If you have programs that go with your exhibit, consider livestreaming them to your followers. Livestreaming is a capacity enabled by social channels to share unedited and raw footage of live events or activities. Recently, the time people spend watching Facebook Live has quadrupled.[8] With the limitation of physical exhibits, live videos break geographic barriers for your users. In addition, tweeting updates and information during the event is a great way to capture your followers' attention and the mood of the event.

Try Paid Ads

If your budget allows it, consider paying for an online ad. Although the prices will vary depending on the specific social media platform, the average cost per click for a Facebook Ad is benchmarked at $1.72.[9] In addition to the regular posts you plan to make, paid ads allow you to target previously untapped audiences.

Pose Questions or Prompts

Start conversations with your followers. Questions or sentence openers relating to a theme or an item from your exhibit can generate chatter. Is there any specific background information that might pique your audience's interest? Are there objects in your exhibit that you want your audience to pay attention to? What did the author or maker of a particular item have to say about their work that might resonate with audiences? Creating a short series of prompts to use throughout your campaign helps remind your audience that your exhibit is still open, and helps you sustain audience interactivity. (See figure 9.3.)

Figure 9.3. Instagram post. *The Robert B. Haas Family Arts Library at Yale University.*

Repurpose Your Content

Perhaps the most important takeaway is this: when using multiple social media platforms, be strategic in your content creation. Use the content you develop for your press release, website, or newsletter to break out into smaller portions and post them on different social media platforms over time.

◎ Definitions

- Hashtag—a word or phrase preceded by a hash sign (#); used on social media websites and applications to identify messages and for easy search on a specific topic

- Livestreaming—a capability enabled by social channels to share unedited and raw footage of live events or activities
- Social Media Influencers—individuals who are known for their expertise on a specific topic and have large followings of their social media activities
- Twitter handle—the username that appears at the end of your unique Twitter URL

⊚ Key Points

- Marketing maximizes the full potential of community impact of your exhibits
- The four marketing stages are research and framing, pre-exhibit marketing, exhibit launch, and post-exhibit marketing
- Use a variety of marketing strategies, including social media channels, online marketing, target marketing, promotional materials, partnerships, and word of mouth to invite your target audience to participate in your library exhibits

⊚ Notes

1. Alman, Susan W. 2018. "Communications, Marketing, and Outreach Strategies." In *Information Services Today: An Introduction*, edited by Sandra Hirsh, 331–42. Lanham, MD: Rowman & Littlefield.

2. Alman, Susan W. 2018. "Communications, Marketing, and Outreach Strategies." In *Information Services Today: An Introduction*, edited by Sandra Hirsh, 331–42. Lanham, MD: Rowman & Littlefield.

3. *American Libraries*. 2009. "The Power of Word-of-Mouth Marketing." Accessed September 1, 2020. https://americanlibrariesmagazine.org/2009/10/26/the-power-of-word-of-mouth -marketing/.

4. Perrin, Andrew, and Monica Anderson. 2019. "Share of U.S. Adults Using Social Media, Including Facebook, Is Mostly Unchanged since 2018." *Pew Research Center*. Accessed September 1, 2020. https://www.pewresearch.org/fact-tank/2019/04/10/share-of-u-s-adults-using-social -media-including-facebook-is-mostly-unchanged-since-2018/.

5. American Library Association. 2014. "Social Networking." Accessed September 1, 2020. http://www.ala.org/news/state-americas-libraries-report-2014/social-networking.

6. Perrin, Andrew, and Monica Anderson. 2019. "Share of U.S. Adults Using Social Media, Including Facebook, Is Mostly Unchanged since 2018." *Pew Research Center*. Accessed September 1, 2020. https://www.pewresearch.org/fact-tank/2019/04/10/share-of-u-s-adults-using-social -media-including-facebook-is-mostly-unchanged-since-2018/.

7. Influencer Marketing Hub. 2020. "What Is an Influencer?" Accessed September 1, 2020. https://influencermarketinghub.com/what-is-an-influencer/.

8. *Facebook for Business*. 2017. "Shifts for 2020: Multisensory Multipliers." Accessed September 1, 2020. https://www.facebook.com/business/news/insights/shifts-for-2020-multisensory -multipliers.

9. Irvin, Mark. 2020. "Facebook Benchmarks for Your Industry [Data]." *Word Stream*. Accessed September 1, 2020. https://www.wordstream.com/blog/ws/2017/02/28/facebook -advertising-benchmarks.

◎ References

Alman, Susan W. 2018. "Communications, Marketing, and Outreach Strategies." In *Information Services Today: An Introduction*, edited by Sandra Hirsh, 331–42. Lanham, MD: Rowman & Littlefield.

American Libraries. 2009. "The Power of Word-of-Mouth Marketing." Accessed September 1, 2020. https://americanlibrariesmagazine.org/2009/10/26/the-power-of-word-of-mouth -marketing/.

American Library Association. 2014. "Social Networking." Accessed September 1, 2020. http://www.ala.org/news/state-americas-libraries-report-2014/social-networking.

Facebook for Business. 2017. "Shifts for 2020: Multisensory Multipliers." Accessed September 1, 2020. https://www.facebook.com/business/news/insights/shifts-for-2020-multisensory -multipliers.

Influencer Marketing Hub. 2020. "What Is an Influencer?" Accessed September 1, 2020. https://influencermarketinghub.com/what-is-an-influencer/.

Irvin, Mark. 2020. "Facebook Benchmarks for Your Industry [Data]." *Word Stream*. Accessed September 1, 2020. https://www.wordstream.com/blog/ws/2017/02/28/facebook-advertising -benchmarks.

Perrin, Andrew, and Monica Anderson. 2019. "Share of U.S. Adults Using Social Media, Including Facebook, Is Mostly Unchanged since 2018." *Pew Research Center*. Accessed September 1, 2020. https://www.pewresearch.org/fact-tank/2019/04/10/share-of-u-s-adults-using-social -media-including-facebook-is-mostly-unchanged-since-2018/.

Resources Mentioned in This Chapter

Online newsletter management applications:

- Constant Contact: www.constantcontact.com/
- Emma: www.myemma.com
- Mailchimp: www.mailchimp.com

◎ Further Reading

Alman, Susan W., and Sara Gillespie Swanson. 2014. *Crash Course in Marketing for Libraries*. 2nd ed. Santa Barbara, CA: Libraries Unlimited.

Barber, Peggy, and Linda Wallace. 2020. *Building a Buzz: Libraries & Word-of-Mouth Marketing*. Chicago: ALA Editions.

Koontz, Christie, and Lorri Mon. 2014. *Marketing and Social Media*. Lanham, MD: Rowman & Littlefield.

Lackie, Robert J., and W. Sandra Wood. 2015. *Creative Library Marketing and Publicity*. Lanham, MD: Rowman & Littlefield.

Ottolenghi, Carol. 2018. *Intentional Marketing: A Practical Guide for Librarians*. Lanham, MD: Rowman & Littlefield.

Public Library Association. 2016. "Marketing Strategies." Accessed September 1, 2020. http://www.ala.org/pla/resources/tools/public-relations-marketing/marketing-strategies.

Siskind, Barry. 2005. *Powerful Exhibit Marketing*. Chicago: John Wiley & Sons.

Assess It!

Audience Evaluation

Why Evaluate?

Evaluation may seem like an unnecessary extra step. You put on the exhibit, people came, and you overheard positive comments. So, you may be asking yourself, "Why evaluate?" We think you should be asking, "Why *not* evaluate?" Evaluation is an integral part of measuring how well and effectively your exhibitions are achieving your goals and how they address the needs of your library users. Similar to any other programs and services your library offers, exhibitions should be user focused. Evaluation enables your library to understand your users and nonusers better, and as a result, improve the services you offer. Evaluation also demonstrates to your users that your library cares about them and their feedback counts.

Libraries are ever-changing organizations, and so are their communities and their users' needs. Evaluation can point out your internal strengths and weaknesses and inform decision-making for future planning and direction setting, which may include other areas of your library's operations, such as collection development and customer services.

Evaluation fosters transparency and trust. With shared evaluation goals, staff, volunteers, and other individuals who are involved in the exhibition will have a heightened awareness of their contribution and build a greater sense of collective ownership of the project. In a sense, evaluation enables your constituents to see the big picture of the work you do at the library, and how exhibits and displays connect with the other parts of the library operations and services. It promotes dialogues for the good of the community and boosts morale and a sense of connectedness from the inside out.

The results from evaluation tell stories about your library's impact. Anecdotal feedback from visitors, attendance statistics, and notes from visitor-interaction observations in the exhibition can illuminate how the exhibition impacts lives. This is especially valuable for exhibitions supported by funding agencies.

Ultimately, evaluation helps libraries attain best practices in user-experience design and delivery, which will advance the organization's mission and values. As you create more exhibition experiences, your accumulated evaluation data allows you to establish standards and benchmarks that can benefit other libraries.

ⓖ Start with the End and Data Collection

Similar to the process of developing programs, you start your evaluation plan with what you would like to see at the end of the exhibition. There are three main stages in the evaluation process: before the exhibition, during the exhibition, and after the exhibition (see table 10.1).

Your choice of data collection is dependent on various factors, including staff support, time, and the scope of the exhibition. Be SMART (Specific, Measurable, Achievable, Relevant, and Timely) in choosing your data collection methods. Ask yourselves these questions to guide your decision-making:

- Specific: Do I know exactly what aspects of audience engagement need to be measured in the exhibit? What are they? Why are they important to the library?
- Measurable: Does the method I choose give me quantified information like numbers and statistics to track the exhibit outcomes?
- Achievable: Do I have sufficient resources—such as time, staffing, space, and money—to implement the method? Do I have what it takes to make it work?
- Relevant: Can this method really show me what I want to know?
- Timely: Can I do this method within the required timeframe?

Before the Exhibition

Before you even start making plans for your exhibition, get your team together and spend time determining how you want to measure audience engagement and exhibition success. Key questions to ask at this stage are the following:

- What are the outcomes we want to see with the exhibition?
- What type of information do we need to gather to reflect the outcomes?
- Is there information from past exhibits that we can use as our baseline?
- If no existing data is available, what would be the best data collection method(s) to gather new information?
- What kind of inputs—such as staffing, time, budget, equipment, or training—do we need to necessitate the desirable outcomes?

Front-End Evaluation

Front-end evaluation is an assessment approach that takes place before an exhibition is opened to the public, with a focus on gathering data about the library users and the exhibition's potential visitors. It can be used to formulate the exhibit elements to address users' needs. If you don't have existing information about your target audience, or the information you have is out-of-date, use front-end evaluation to inform your decision-making when you begin planning your exhibition.

To collect data, here are the methods that can be easily and quickly adopted with minimal financial and staffing requirements, and show a relatively high return on investment:

- Conduct a survey about your users, either by e-mail or on-site. The questions may range from demographics and knowledge background, to open-ended questions about their interests.
- Interview your users. This is more labor-intensive and time-consuming but allows you to capture in-depth and idiosyncratic information for your evaluation.
- Facilitate focus groups. Similar to conducting interviews, this also requires time and staff support to yield results.
- Crowdsource ideas from your users on-site using participatory activities, such as comment boxes, Post-it notes, and polls
- Talk informally with library users

Formative Evaluation

With a focus on identifying concerns or challenges in order to make necessary adjustments to the exhibition to enhance visitors' engagement, formative evaluation is an assessment approach that takes place once an exhibition is open to the public. This evaluation method is particularly relevant for non-traveling exhibitions or larger-scale in-house exhibition projects. Here, you continuously seek feedback from your target audience on how well the proposed exhibition communicates your intended message as you develop the exhibition content. At this stage, trial and error is expected, as you are developing exhibit programming. Methods for formative evaluation include the following:

- Making prototypes and testing the exhibit elements with a select group of potential users to refine the exhibition
- Soliciting feedback from staff or other library peers

During the Exhibition

Evaluation should occur during the exhibition because you want to maximize its impact and provide timely responses to any issues that potentially impede your ability to reach exhibit goals. During the exhibit you will gather data for later analysis to help answer the evaluation questions, and throughout the exhibit you will continuously monitor exhibition quality and audience engagement to ensure you are meeting goals. Key questions to ask are these:

- Does the exhibition work the way it is intended to?
- How are the visitors responding to the exhibit?

- What challenges or difficulties are visitors experiencing? What causes these challenges?

Remedial Evaluation

Remedial evaluation is a process to troubleshoot unexpected problems and react with adjustments to improve the visitors' exhibit experiences. It takes place while the exhibit is open to the public. Your focus is on checking how the exhibition functions and how your users respond to it. You determine if additional resources are needed to correct any issues.

Data collection methods can involve the following:

- Team meetings to monitor and assess how well your exhibition is received and discuss ways to adjust and improve your exhibition if needed
- Direct observation of visitor behaviors by staff or volunteers—for example, measuring and analyzing visitors' "dwell time"—time they spent at a given exhibit component or location

After the Exhibition

When your exhibition is completed and closed, you evaluate outcomes and impact. Key questions to ask are these:

- Did we meet our exhibition goals? Why or why not?
- Did we meet our library users' needs? Why or why not?
- What were the unexpected outcomes? What surprised us?
- What lessons did we learn from this exhibition? What did we learn about our target audience, the execution of our exhibit production, and our marketing efforts and programming?

Summative Evaluation

With a focus on gathering data that demonstrates the impact and effectiveness of the exhibition, summative evaluation is an assessment approach that takes place after the exhibition is completed. The results from summative evaluation provide valuable insights for future exhibit planning. The data will cycle back and feed your front-end evaluation for your next exhibit project.

Data collection methods may involve the following:

- Surveying exhibit visitors and exhibit program participants on their overall experience
- Soliciting feedback from staff and other library peers
- Gathering comments with a guestbook
- Counting number of visitors/participants
- If you have in-gallery activities or takeaways at the exhibit, measuring supplies used or books circulated
- Tracking the number and types of questions about your exhibit that you receive at your reference desk and via social media

Table 10.1. Data Collection Method Matrix

	BEFORE THE EXHIBITION	DURING THE EXHIBITION	AFTER THE EXHIBITION
Front-End Evaluation	Survey Interview Focus group Informal conversations Crowdsourcing ideas		
Formative Evaluation	Prototyping and testing Informal conversations		
Remedial Evaluation		Time meetings Staff and peer feedback Direct observation and dwell time	
Summative Evaluation			Survey Staff and peer feedback Guestbook comments Head counts Measuring supplies used or books circulated Reference questions asked Website analytics Social media reactions (likes, shares, and comments) Press and media coverage

Carol Ng-He.

- Using analytics to track online visitorship or patterns for online content related to the exhibition
- Tracking related news features, reviews, and other press and media coverage

An example of a summative survey can be found in the resources section at the end of this chapter.

Organizing the Data

Once you've collected data, you should begin to organize, collate, and digitize the information in a centralized location for easy retrieval and comparison. Make sure you also back up your files.

Typically, data can be either quantitative (e.g., number of visitors) or qualitative (e.g., guest book comments). As you go over your data, consider using a spreadsheet to process, sort, and reconfigure the information to help reveal trends and patterns and any unexpected results. Make note of them for your report.

As an old saying goes, "Sharing is caring." Sharing your evaluation results is an act of caring for the work you do. Think about who will read your report and find out what they want or need to know. Think about the level of detail and breadth of results you will share with your audience and choose your form of presentation accordingly. Your presentation can be a summary in a newsletter (print or electronic), blog post, written report, slideshow, video, or an oral presentation at staff or board meetings, and even conference presentations. To enhance the visual appeal of your report, create infographics about your attendance, outputs, and related exhibition outcomes, as well as photos of the exhibition and its visitors.

After you present the report, you may receive additional feedback about the exhibition that can be applied when you plan your next exhibition. If applicable, you and your team may want to share with your administration relevant feedback on areas relating to the library's daily operations and infrastructure.

To wrap up this chapter, we invited four librarians to share their experiences and reflections on evaluation. The librarians work in a variety of library settings: an art museum library, a state library, an independent research library, and an academic library. Each of them has had different experiences evaluating exhibits, which has affected their hopes and dreams for implementing evaluation in the future.

Doug Litts, Former Executive Director
Ryerson and Burnham Libraries, Art Institute of Chicago

Why does the library do exhibitions?

The primary goal is to expose items in the library's collections to the museum visitors. Often we have exhibitions that tie to the museum galleries' happenings. Our staff also volunteer to create exhibitions on themes based on their personal interests. The production of the library exhibitions is spread across departments at the museum, including the label text vetting by Interpretation in the Learning and Public Engagement Department, editing by the Publishing Department, and object condition assessment and mounting as needed by the Conservation and Science Department.

How do you know if you have met your exhibition goals?

Our library exhibitions are treated as a rotation at the museum, which means that there is no evaluation per se. Because our goal is simple (collection exposure), our exhibitions are not meant to be didactic like those in the museum galleries. Mainly we evaluate our exhibitions by keeping track of the traffic numbers and observing the visitors' browsing in the exhibition.

What are hindrances, challenges, or issues you face in implementing exhibition evaluation?

Before considering conducting an evaluation, there are physical challenges for us to do exhibitions in our library, such as a lack of vitrines (glass display cases) proportionally sized to certain items, a lack of availability of librarian-curators, competing priorities at the library, and little control over the room lighting because it's a historical landmark. With our current exhibition efforts, while implementing evaluation is not a priority for us, I would be curious to learn how it is done in the museum galleries and see how they would be of interest to us. I'd love to find out what visitors take away from visiting our exhibitions.

What would help you overcome these challenges?

Funding and staff support would be necessary. Currently, no budget is dedicated to the library exhibitions, and staff carve out time from their existing duties to develop exhibitions. Ideally, the involvement of external contributors at the museum outside of the curatorial departments would be a great way to rejuvenate the exhibition space and broaden public engagement with the exhibitions.

Andrew Bullen, Information Technology Coordinator
Illinois State Library

What is your goal for evaluation for your exhibitions?

My goal is to find out the best way to present data from the Illinois Digital Archives.

Who is typically involved in conducting the evaluation?

Myself. I am passionate about CONTENTdm (a digital collection management system). Because the [Illinois] State Library is quite new to doing exhibitions of materials, our focus has been on getting collections published, and less on building, evaluating, and planning exhibitions with the materials in the collections. However, ideally, I see that we would work with the state archives, and utilize their collections to build a narrative and develop exhibition efforts.

How often do you conduct evaluation per exhibition?

Once. For example, in one exhibition program that I put together, *Won't You Be a Part? Pullman in the First World War* (see figure 10.1), held at the Pullman State Historic Site in Chicago in 2016, I

Figure 10.1. Photograph from *Won't You Be a Part? Pullman in the First World War* in the original Pullman Factory building, Chicago. *Andrew Bullen.*

handed out survey postcards with just three questions: Did you enjoy the performance? Was the way the images were presented useful? How would you like us to improve the presentation for the future? At the end of the presentation, I also showed a link to the same survey on SurveyMonkey and had it opened for two weeks to solicit additional responses.

What surprises you when you do an evaluation?

For this exhibit program, I was surprised by how many people commented on it, and that more positive and informative feedback was collected from the postcards than from SurveyMonkey. The direct and immediate feelings as experienced on-site might have helped the participants find an outlet to express it and the postcards were at the right place at the right time for them to do it.

Amanda Cacich, Assistant Registrar and Exhibition Specialist Newberry Library

What is your goal for evaluation?

We're still actively defining what our goals are for evaluation. In the past, we've asked very standard demographic questions like age, gender, education level, et cetera. We've also asked broad questions, such as, "What could be improved about this exhibit?" While demographic information is good, we're interested in delving deeper into how people interact with our exhibits, and how it affects their relationship with the institution as a whole.

Who is typically involved in conducting the evaluation?

Usually, evaluation is pretty passive. I will put out a binder of our standard exhibit surveys, which are the same for every exhibit. This survey is where we ask the questions I mentioned above. Once a number of surveys are filled out, I'll record the data in a spreadsheet, and I keep doing this throughout the run of the exhibition. We also have people counters, installed throughout the galleries, that give us an idea of general attendance. In the future, we would like to train volunteers to do direct observation in the galleries and in-person surveys.

How long do you conduct evaluation per exhibition?

We begin counting attendance numbers and putting out surveys on the opening date of the exhibition and stop collecting this data on the closing date.

What surprises you when you do an evaluation?

Conflicting views expressed by different visitors always surprise me. For example, one visitor will say there were too many maps in the exhibit, and another visitor will want to see even more maps. It's interesting how two people can attend the same exhibition and have such opposing reactions.

How do you analyze and apply your evaluation results for future planning?

During a few of our previous exhibitions, we received feedback via the surveys that the galleries had limited mobility and were overcrowded with cases. In recent exhibitions, we've worked to cut back the number of items on display and ensure that there is 36 inches (the ADA recommended amount) between cases. Another thing we've noticed is the importance of a strong exhibition identity. When the exhibition subject is too vague, people get confused and don't understand the message. Past exhibit surveys have demonstrated this general confusion among visitors, so we know to have very clear and understandable exhibition topics in the future.

Megan Lotts, Art Librarian
Rutgers University Libraries

What is your goal when evaluating?

At the Rutgers Art Library (RAL), one of the goals from the exhibits program is to find out what library users learn or gain from these spaces. Also, the libraries want to provide space for students to show their scholarly work. When I was an art student, I found that there was a lack of exhibit space for student artists. As an art librarian, I see a lack in art students using the art library. Therefore, at RAL, the exhibition spaces address both issues. Exhibition evaluation is not just about pretty pictures and numbers; it's about gaining an understanding of exhibits as a method of learning and engagement, as well as a means to highlight collections. In the end, RAL wants to engage their communities and provide resources and experiences that encourage our users to learn more.

How long do you conduct evaluation per exhibition?

RAL has a variety of ways in which they evaluate exhibits and these processes begin from the moment a proposal is "brought to the table" and can last for months after an exhibit physically ends—in particular, if there is a virtual aspect to the exhibit (see figure 10.2). Evaluation and assessment do not end when a program or exhibit is over. Ideally an impactful exhibit leaves a lasting effect, such as users wanting more and a desire to continue the conversation.

Figure 10.2. Rutgers University Libraries' digital exhibition *Fluxes. Rutgers University Libraries.*

How do you determine what evaluation measure works best for your library?

RAL has a menu of ways in which they evaluate events, exhibits, and programming. This includes multiple entry points depending on the methods of evaluation chosen for each exhibit and sometimes this is determined by time and staff availability. However, assessment and evaluation methods are chosen once the goals of an exhibit have been specified. If you don't have a goal, exhibits can be much harder to evaluate. Also, RAL tries to keep the exhibition program low-cost and efficient by using tools and skills sets that are widely present among staff, as well as by regularly evaluating the exhibition program as a whole to see what is working and what is not.

What are your evaluation methods?

RAL has a range of methods when it comes to assessment that are chosen based on [the] scope and content of each individual exhibit. This can include:

- Surveys, count numbers of patrons, supplies used, reference questions asked, and more
- Monitoring social media and local media sources to collect comments, likes, shares, or stories about one's event or project
- If there is extra time and help, someone captures comments overheard, questions asked, and interesting engagement or connections made among patrons—in particular, engagement between different disciplines or departments within an organization
- Document with digital image, sound, and video, which can be tricky depending on your organization's policies involving documentation of patrons, and some people simply do not like their photo taken. Sometimes documentation can only be used for internal purposes.
- Collect any leftover ephemera from the event or project, such as completed or uncompleted activities, brainstorming pages, notes, flip charts, et cetera
- Have a comment box or means to leave a virtual comment

But, perhaps most importantly, after each exhibit the Rutgers University Libraries—New Brunswick (RUL-NB) has an assessment form which serves as a mini-debriefing and provides a space to write about what did and did not work and what the impact of the exhibit/program/service was. This form also provides RUL-NB insight into what is happening within the organization. This larger body of information can help with future planning, especially when budgets and staff are dwindling. As well, information gleaned from this form helps tell our story and show impact for reports to administrators, funders, and more.

Who is typically involved in conducting the evaluation?

At Rutgers, whoever coordinates an event is in charge of the assessment. In the Art Library, I have a student worker who supports reference and instruction within RAL for six hours a week during the fall and spring semesters. Their skill set dictates their engagement in evaluation. For example, sometimes student workers curate an exhibition, which includes assessment.

What surprises you about evaluation?

The most exciting aspects of an exhibit can be in the assessment of it. One learns about interesting comments or stories, unexpected connections visitors make, and I love hearing about first time visitors to RAL—in particular, when they note they will likely be back.

⊚ Definitions

- Evaluation—the process of collecting, analyzing, interpreting, and reporting data from an exhibition or related project
- Formative evaluation—an assessment approach that takes place once an exhibition is open, with a focus on identifying concerns or challenges in order to make necessary adjustments to the exhibition to enhance visitor engagement
- Front-end evaluation—an assessment approach that takes place before an exhibition is opened to the public, with a focus on gathering data about library users and the exhibition's potential visitors. It can be used to formulate exhibit elements to address user needs.
- Remedial evaluation—a process to troubleshoot unexpected problems to improve visitor experiences
- Summative evaluation—an assessment approach that takes place after the exhibition is completed, with a focus on gathering data that demonstrates the impact and effectiveness of the exhibition. The results from this type of evaluation can become front-end evaluation for future exhibitions.

⊚ Key Points

- Evaluation is an essential part of exhibition planning
- There are three main stages of evaluation: before the exhibition, during the exhibition, and after the exhibition. Each stage involves different types of evaluation, including front-end evaluation, formative evaluation, remedial evaluation, and summative evaluation.
- The choice of data collection is dependent on various factors, including staff support, time, and the scope of the exhibition. Libraries should evaluate using SMART (Specific, Measurable, Achievable, Relevant, and Timely) goals.
- Analyzing and interpreting data is important, as it reveals trends and patterns and unexpected outcomes that are useful for future planning
- Report and respond to the evaluation results to improve the library's operations and services

⊚ References

Counts, Charity, and, Trici O'Connora. 2019. "Creative Ways to Move Ideas Forward in Exhibit Projects Workshop Series: Seeking Audience Input to Build an Effective Exhibit Lineup Workshop Toolkit." (Handout received in Strategies for Exhibit Content Development webinar, May 10, 2019.)

Lotts, Megan. 2018. "Outreach, Engagement, and Highlighting the Rutgers University Libraries Collections." Rutgers University Libraries. Accessed September 1, 2020. https://doi.org/doi:10.7282/T3CN77CJ.

McKenna-Cress, Polly, and Janet A. Kamien. 2013. *Creating Exhibitions: Collaboration in the Planning, Development, and Design of Innovative Experiences.* Hoboken, NJ: John Wiley & Sons.

Renaissance East of England. 2018. *Evaluation Toolkit from Museum Practitioners.* Norwich, UK: East of England Museum Hub. Accessed September 1, 2020. http://visitors.org.uk/wp-content/uploads/2014/08/ShareSE_Evaltoolkit.pdf.

Walhimer, Mark. 2012. "Museum Exhibition Design, Part VI." *Museum Planner* (blog). Accessed September 1, 2020. https://museumplanner.org/museum-exhibition-design-part-vi/.

Resources Mentioned in This Chapter

EVENTS, EXHIBITS, OUTREACH, AND ENGAGEMENT ASSESSMENT FORM, RUTGERS UNIVERSITY LIBRARIES— NEW BRUNSWICK LIBRARIES (NBL)

*Required

1. Name of RUL faculty or staff member coordinating or attending event, outreach, or engagement?*

2. Location where the event took place?* (e.g., Art Library or CAC student center)

3. Type of event, outreach, or engagement?* (Mark only one oval)

   Orientation—Any orientation or welcome activity. Orientations may include tables at information fairs, library tours, presentations during larger orientation programs.
   Outreach—Any event that originates from the library/library-initiated, including author talks, exhibits, and film screenings.
   Partnership—Any event (not including orientations to groups outside the libraries) that is co-sponsored with the library functioning as one participating partner.
   Other:

4. Name of event, outreach, or engagement?*

5. Did you also record this in the BI Stats database?* (Mark only one oval) Yes/ No

6. Date this event, outreach, or engagement took place?

7. Time this event, outreach, or engagement took place?*

8. Do you have a flyer(s)? (up to 10 MB and no more than 5 files)

9. Please list partner(s) below including any contact information?

10. Were there any sponsor(s)?

11. Target population?* (Check all that apply)

    Undergraduate students
    Graduate students

Faculty
Other:

12. Did you highlight a Rutgers University Libraries service or collection?

13. Did this tie back to the NBL's Strategic Plan? (Check all that apply)

    Goal 1: Empower Student Success
    Goal 2: Strengthen Faculty and Graduate Student Research and Teaching
    Goal 3: Build Connections
    Other:

14. Number of attendees?

15. Please share any comments about assessment of this event, outreach, or engagement.*

16. Please upload any assessment documents you would like to share. (ex., spreadsheet of surveys, Microsoft Word document, or other) (up to 10 MB)

17. Do you have any pictures from the event, outreach, or engagement? (up to 10 MB and no more than 10 files)

18. Please provide any additional comments about this event you would like to share including impact, stories from the event, etc.

EXHIBITION AND EVENT EVALUATION FORM, RUTGERS UNIVERSITY LIBRARIES— NEW BRUNSWICK LIBRARIES (NBL)

The Art Library Wants to Know . . .

How did you learn about this exhibit/event?

What did you like about this exhibit/event?

What other activities would you like to see at the Art Library?

What is the time you would most like to see events happen in the Art Library?

How would you like to hear about Art Library exhibitions/events?

⊚ Further Reading

Bradburn, Norman, Timothy Johnson, Michael Stern, and Brian Wansink. 2004. *Asking Questions: The Definitive Guide to Questionnaire Design*. San Francisco: Jossey-Bass.

Diamond, Judy, Jessica J. Luke, and David H. Uttal. 2009. *Practical Evaluation Guide: Tools for Museums and Other Informal Educational Settings*. Walnut Creek, CA: AltaMira Press.

Friedman, Alan, ed. 2008. *Framework for Evaluating Impacts of Informal Science Education Projects: Report from a National Science Foundation Workshop*. The National Science Foundation. Accessed September 1, 2020. https://www.informalscience.org/sites/default/files/Eval_Framework.pdf.

Lacher-Feldman, Jessica. 2013. *Exhibits in Archives and Special Collections Libraries*. Chicago: The Society of American Archivists.

Serrell, Beverly. 2017. *Judging Exhibitions: A Framework for Assessing Excellence*. Abingdon, UK: Routledge.

Bibliography

Alliance for Networking Visual Culture. "About Scalar." Accessed September 1, 2020. https://scalar.me/anvc/.

Alman, Susan W. 2018. "Communications, Marketing, and Outreach Strategies." In *Information Services Today: An Introduction*, 2nd ed., edited by Sandra Hirsh, 331–42. Lanham, MD: Rowman & Littlefield.

American Libraries. 2009. "The Power of Word-of-Mouth Marketing." Accessed September 1, 2020. https://americanlibrariesmagazine.org/2009/10/26/the-power-of-word-of-mouth-marketing/.

American Library Association. 2014. "Social Networking." Accessed September 1, 2020. http://www.ala.org/news/state-americas-libraries-report-2014/social-networking.

Bachmann, Konstanze. 2012. *Conservations Concerns: A Guide for Collectors and Curators*. Washington, DC: Smithsonian Books.

Brim, Richenda. 2001. "From Custodians to Disseminators: Libraries and Digital Exhibitions." Howard Besser's webpage. Accessed September 1, 2020. http://besser.tsoa.nyu.edu/impact/f01/Papers/Brim/digi_ex.htm.

Brown, Mary E., and Rebecca Power. 2006. *Exhibits in Libraries: A Practical Guide*. Jefferson, NC: McFarland.

City Lights Pocket Poets eries 1955–2005: From the Collection of Donald A. Henneghan. October 1, 2005–January 1, 2006. Special Collections Research Center, University of Chicago Library, Chicago.

Counts, Charity, and O'Connor, Tricia. 2019. "Creative Ways to Move Ideas Forward in Exhibit Projects Workshop Series: Seeking Audience Input to Build an Effective Exhibit Lineup Workshop Toolkit." (Handout received in Strategies for Exhibit Content Development webinar, May 10, 2019.)

Duke University. "WCAG Principles and Guidelines." Accessed September 1, 2020. https://web.accessibility.duke.edu/learn/wcag-guidelines.

eNews Park Forest. 2017. "National Veterans Art Museum Announces Events in Honor of Memorial Day 2017." Accessed September 1, 2020. https://www.enewspf.com/opinion/blog-posts/national-veterans-art-museum-announces-events-honor-memorial-day-2017/.

Facebook for Business. 2017. "Shifts for 2020: Multisensory Multipliers." Accessed September 1, 2020. https://www.facebook.com/business/news/insights/shifts-for-2020-multisensory-multipliers.

Gewirtz, Isaac. 2009. *Kerouac at Bat: Fantasy Sports and the King of the Beats*. New York: New York Public Library.

Gibbons, Patti. 2015. "Disaster Management and Exhibition Loans: Contingency Planning for Items on Display." In *Handbook of Research on Disaster Management and Contingency Planning in Modern Libraries*, edited by E. Decker and J. Townes. Hershey, PA: IGI-Global.

Hansen, Beth. 2017. *Great Exhibits! An Exhibit Planning and Construction Handbook for Small Museums*. Lanham, MD: AltaMira Press.

Hildebrandt, Beth, Stacey Knight-Davis, J. J. Pionke, and Andrew Cougill. 2019. "Designs of Duty: Using Exhibits to Build Partnerships." *College & Undergraduate Libraries*. 26 (1): 52–65.

Influencer Marketing Hub. 2020. "What Is an Influencer?" Accessed September 1, 2020. https://influencermarketinghub.com/what-is-an-influencer/.

Irvin, Mark. 2020. "Facebook Benchmarks for Your Industry [Data]." *Word Stream*. Accessed September 1, 2020. https://www.wordstream.com/blog/ws/2017/02/28/facebook-advertising-benchmarks.

Kobayashi, Evelyn, and MaryJoy Rojo. 2018. "A Small Library's Playbook for Hosting NLM Traveling Exhibits." *Journal of Hospital Librarianship*. 18 (1): 38–46.

Lord, Barry, and Gail Dexter Lord, eds. 2002. *The Manual of Museum Exhibitions*. Walnut Creek, CA: AltaMira Press.

Lotts, Megan. 2016. "Building Bridges, Creating Partnerships, and Elevating the Arts: The Rutgers University Art Library Exhibition Spaces." *College & Research Libraries News*. 77 (5): 226–30.

Lotts, Megan. 2018. "Outreach, Engagement, and Highlighting the Rutgers University Libraries Collections." Rutgers University Libraries. Accessed September 1, 2020. https://doi.org/doi:10.7282/T3CN77CJ.

Matassa, Freda. 2011. *Museum Collections Management*. London: Facet Publishing.

McKenna-Cress, Polly, and Janet A. Kamien. 2013. *Creating Exhibitions: Collaboration in the Planning, Development, and Design of Innovative Experiences*. Hoboken, NJ: John Wiley & Sons.

Northeast Document Conservation Center. 1999. "2.5 Protecting Paper and Book Collections during Exhibition." Accessed September 1, 2020. https://www.nedcc.org/free-resources/preservation-leaflets/2.-the-environment/2.5-protecting-paper-and-book-collections-during-exhibition.

Northeast Document Conservation Center. 2012. "2.4 Protection from Light Damage." Accessed September 1, 2020. https://www.nedcc.org/free-resources/preservation-leaflets/2.-the-environment/2.4-protection-from-light-damage.

O'Donnell, Kerry. 2017. "How Do Library Displays Happen?" The Public Library of Brookline. Accessed September 1, 2020. https://www.brooklinelibrary.org/2017/04/20/how-do-library-displays-happen/.

Open Education Database. "5 Free and Open Source Tools for Creating Web Exhibitions." Accessed September 1, 2020. https://oedb.org/ilibrarian/5-free-and-open-source-tools-for-creating-digital-exhibitions/.

Palmer, Ada. 2018. *Censorship and Information Control*. September 17, 2018–December 14, 2018. Special Collections Research Center, University of Chicago Library, Chicago.

Perrin, Andrew, and Monica Anderson. 2019. "Share of U.S. Adults Using Social Media, Including Facebook, Is Mostly Unchanged since 2018." Pew Research Center. Accessed September 1, 2020. https://www.pewresearch.org/fact-tank/2019/04/10/share-of-u-s-adults-using-social-media-including-facebook-is-mostly-unchanged-since-2018/.

Reidsma, Matthew. 2014. *Responsive Web Design for Libraries: A LITA Guide*. Chicago: ALA TechSource.

Renaissance East of England. 2018. *Evaluation Toolkit from Museum Practitioners*. Norwich, UK: East of England Museum Hub. Accessed September 1, 2020. http://visitors.org.uk/wp-content/uploads/2014/08/ShareSE_Evaltoolkit.pdf.

Rush, Sharron. 2013. "Why Web Accessibility Matters for Cultural Institutions: Overview of Legal Requirements, Typical Problems, Practical Guidelines and Examples of Website

Redesign." New York: Art Beyond Site. Accessed September 1, 2020. http://www.artbeyond
  sight.org/mei/wp-content/uploads/WP_MSWEB.pdf.

Salina Journal. 2019. "Salina Public Library to Host Pop-Up Mobile Museum." Accessed September 1, 2020. https://www.salina.com/news/20190703/salina-public-library-to-host-pop
  -up-mobile-museum.

Serrell, Beverly. 2015. *Exhibition Labels: An Interpretive Approach.* Lanham, MD: Rowman & Littlefield.

Smithsonian Exhibits. 2018. *A Guide to Exhibit Development.* Landover, MD: Smithsonian Exhibits.

Smithsonian Institution. 1996. *Smithsonian Guidelines for Accessible Exhibition Design.* Washington, DC: Smithsonian Accessibility Program. Accessed September 1, 2020. https://www
  .sifacilities.si.edu/sites/default/files/Files/Accessibility/accessible-exhibition-design1.pdf.

Smithsonian Institution. [2016]. *Museum on Main Street: Storytelling Toolkit.* Washington, DC: Smithsonian Institution. PDF e-publication. Accessed September 1, 2020. https://museum
  onmainstreet.org/search/node/storytelling%20toolkit.

Stim, Richard. 2016. *Getting Permission: Using & Licensing Copyright-Protected Materials Online & Off.* Berkeley, CA: Nolo.

Stiteler, Gretchen. 2019. "Penn Museum Library Shares Rare Books in Monthly Pop-Up Exhibits." *Penn Libraries News.* Accessed September 1, 2020. https://www.library.upenn.edu/blogs/
  libraries-news/2019/05/29/5928.

The Sketchbook Project. "Work with the Sketchbook Project." Accessed September 1, 2020. https://www.sketchbookproject.com/exhibitions.

The University of Chicago Press. 2017. *The Chicago Manual of Style Online.* 17th ed. Accessed September 1, 2020. https://www.chicagomanualofstyle.org/home.html.

Walhimer, Mark. 2012. "Museum Exhibition Design, Part VI." *Museum Planner* (blog). Accessed September 1, 2020. https://museumplanner.org/museum-exhibition-design-part-vi/.

World Wide Web Consortium (W3C). 2008. "Web Content Accessibility Guidelines (WCAG) 2.0." Accessed September 1, 2020. https://www.w3.org/TR/WCAG20/.

Index

Page references for figures are italicized